Achieve Financial Freedom

A Modern Guide To Personal Growth, Strategic Budgeting, And Wealth Building For Beginners

By

Chalondra A. J. Maxwell

Copyright

Disclaimer

This book is meant for general information and education. The author worked hard for accuracy, but there's no surety it's complete, reliable, current, or error-free.
The author isn't giving professional advice or services. What's here isn't a replacement for talking

to pros in that field. The author isn't responsible for what you do based on the info here.

There might be mentions of other sources, websites, or services, but the author doesn't back or guarantee their accuracy, relevance, timeliness, or completeness. The author and publisher don't take responsibility for what those other places say or do. Stories of success or testimonials in this book are about individual experiences. They're not a sure thing for any reader.

Using this book and the info in it is your choice and your risk. You're the one responsible for what you do based on this book, and the author won't be blamed for any harm or losses from using it.

About The Author

Chalondra A. J. Maxwell is a writer, speaker and business personality when it comes to personal development, finance, and business strategy. Chalondra has devoted her life mission to equipping people with skills that help them achieve financial stability and self-actualization.

The fact that she has done it, indicates how hard she was in pursuit of success. She had a degree in finance and knew the inner dynamics of the financial system. She not only amassed wealth for herself but has improved many people's lives through this knowledge and experience.

Besides the writing, Chalondra A. J. Maxwell is an in demand motivator who addresses different levels of self-actualization speaking on the podiums. This has made her one of the most revered figures in the areas of financial education and personal development because of her magnetic presence on stage and ability to relate with audiences at a deeper level.

Chalondra A. J. Maxwell remains a powerful voice in the sphere of personal development and financial emancipation. These could hold the key to the realization of our success and self-actualization as individuals, societies, countries, regions and the world as a whole.

Table Of Contents

Introductions

People seek success so often; it remains one of the most unrealized goals. One of the many obstacles that people face along their success journey involves abandoning the struggle once they endure temporary losing.

This is a rather common mistake that most people have fallen victim to. People wish to build their fortunes and become financially stable but many who fail do so on account of allowing other people's thoughts or sentiments dictate them.

Their reason is that they allow neighbors' gossip as well as newspaper information to drive their thoughts. However, it should be noted that these perspectives are exactly those cheapest things any person who is willing to get them can find.

However, this question is centered on whether our viewpoints influence decision making. In addition, it becomes harder for us to succeed in any endeavor once we let ourselves be guided by external forces.

Especially with reference to how to convert private aims into financial profit. Building a mansion is like financial success and personal development. A mansion cannot be built if it lacks a strong base. They have laid out hope's expectations and a desire to live rather than just be alive.

In present times, many opportunities and challenges cross paths, making the roads towards personal growth and financial independence look easy, yet hard to reach.

In a world where access has no boundaries, with information right there by your fingertips and a world right at the doorsteps, it will seem like getting to your financial peak while achieving maximum personal development is as easy as a walk in the park.

However, searching for genuine, sincere satisfaction in a realm that consists of unlimited selections amidst perpetual diversions might be likened to steering one's way through the complexities.

On a daily basis, we trudge through an obstacle course of digital notifications as we rush to complete individual duties and digital responsibilities before reaching the end goal post.

This uninterrupted bombardment of advertisements, endless noise from social media platforms, and constant pursuit for our attention might end up making us separated from our inner souls.

Dear reader, join me in taking this road that merges up-to-date events. An adventure, which requires disengaging from the continuous cycle of everyday life and allocating time for inner contemplation. These times of introspection will allow you to start unraveling the complicated knot of your goals, needs, and socio-interpersonal influences. Through these outer influences you will find yourself and not as self-indulgence but self-empowerment.

This is because it recognizes the route of finding real monetary freedom as well as enduring personal development, which is the knowledge of who one truly is. Following social norms should be secondary and matching a path with an individual's inner compass should be prioritized. However, my objective in this voyage is not to promise any overnight successful solutions or quick fixes.

Alternatively, I write my own complete and applicable handbook on how to become wealthy drawing from the wellspring of human learning and wisdom of current experience.

Therefore, my intention cannot be better captured as one that seeks to illuminate upon a path whose twists and turns not acceptable lead to massive transformations at the end. Your brain will be transformed as you discover the importance of a growth mindset for personal change; master self-appreciation as you develop an escape plan from constricted notions.

I'll discuss thoroughly the possible methods of revenue collection, debt repayment, and budgeting respectively.

This trip is more about self-awareness, enlightenment, and metamorphosis rather than immediate pleasure. Hence, let us jointly move through the intricacies of modern living to trace the true paths towards self-satisfaction and wealth. The journey towards financial success has other benefits other than financial gain. It has the purpose of helping you discover meaning in life and live it the way it should be lived; as a success.

Scan this QR code to discover more about the author!
Visit the Author Central page for exclusive insights and
updates on more invaluable books.

Chapter 1

Unleashing Your Potentials

There is a whisper deep inside everyone, indicating that there is a special talent in us which can change the world to be for the best. One day in our life, we looked forward into the future dreaming of the kind of life that we wanted to live.

However, year after year, people lose their interest to do so because they become involved in everyday battles, and these dreams are entangled in this web, thus it is difficult to achieve. However, as our initial enthusiasm subsides so does our willingness to control the life we want. I have spent all my life working towards finding ways to realize those dreams for myself and everyone around me, each of us possesses untapped ability.

Contemplate your history. What were your dreams then? What did you imagine for yourself in the future?

Have you achieved any steps closer to materializing those dreams?

Did those objectives that you projected at the beginning bear any fruits in the course of your life?

The ability to act provides the transformational agent for shaping our destinies. The only real difference between those outcomes is in the choices we made, and our willingness to take those steps. Each event is like dropping a stone into water whereby it reverberates, leading to an unpredictable series of processes.

As a result, each individual action forms part of this trail and path which guides each of us, on the journey where we are writing our own fate.

Discovering Your True Self

Life's winding search for the self you seek. Such a search forms the basis for one's growth as an individual, as well as for wealth creation. All other quests lie below it. So, see this voyage as a treasure trail looking for the actual, uncontaminated you in lieu of diamonds and gold. To find this treasure, use the inner compass within your soul, and not the physical maps or coordinates. You discover your inner strength, self-respect, and self-knowledge on such voyages.

Discovering your true identity is something which occurs throughout a long-term period and happens continuously. This starts as an interruption in daily life and asking yourself "Who am I really?".
It marks the commencement of a voyage that may be strenuous but always rewarding. It's the journey of discovering yourself that goes beyond your daily life activities and the labels assigned by society. It is essentially an examination of your values, motivations, and heart's desires.

More often than not, society and social expectations make us forget who we truly are. We portray the personalities and acts that actually do not correspond with our real self, hence we become as the others want us to be.

These acts of divorce could be those reasons why we feel lost, depressed and clueless. The accumulated peer pressure, self-doubts, and cultural conditioning over many years must be stripped off in order for you to get back to yourself. It is about shedding the masks you put on in order to please others or fulfill expectations. This process is like the removal of old skin and coming out with a new, immaculate self.

When examining the intricacies of true self, your true self might depart from what society expects or even norms. That is fine since it could be strange. The real "you" is just one manifestation of who you truly are and not bound by conventions set up by society.

One of its most beautiful aspects is that finding for yourself your own true self would allow you to live a life as if you are living out your true passion and value. It helps you feel that you have a purpose and it is aligned with what you really wish for in life. It is this alignment that provides fuel for your journey toward business and personal success.

In the following chapters, you will find out that this path of self-discovering is not a solo mission. It goes hand in hand with your financial progression. Your financial goals become more profound when they are influenced by who you are and what you feel at this point in life. Your quest for financial gains turns into something genuine that you are not doing as part of social obligation alone.

Hence, understanding who you become during this life-transforming journey is a continuous process and not a destination. On this journey, you will find traits of yourself not known before. This is how you can achieve maximal realization of your potential, be successful financially, live a full life filled with high emotions and express yourself as you really are.

Unlocking Your True Self: 14 Routes To Self-Discovery

Introspection

Among these, introspection is one of the most powerful tools to discover oneself. Such practice is a reflection that requires self-auditing of thought, emotions, and behavior. In a way, it's like being your own detective, investigating the patterns and motives that drive your actions.

In its purest sense, introspection is the ability to look into oneself to achieve a deep understanding of what one thinks, feels, or has experienced. It is a way of going into the darkest parts of your inner thoughts, contemplations, thinking and perceptions.

Introspection may be cast aside due to the dynamic nature of the fast changing contemporary world but this is what helps you realize who you really are. The diary helps clear up the confusion resulting from ideas and emotions, by looking through them, identifying your actions' patterns, exploring your deepest desires and fears as well as finding out the reasons behind the occurrences in your life.

Self discovery heavily relies upon introspection. This opportunity enables one to understand what one really loves in life and accept it. It's about development, not criticism. Introspection helps you observe your own living while analyzing your emotions and thoughts in an objective manner.

You can do this by dedicating a few minutes every day for quiet self-reflection. Select a quiet place, do not litter, and focus on mindful thinking. This requires no sophisticated equipment or techniques. Simply stay in the present. Embrace introspection as an important friend in your quest for self-awareness.

Find some personal time and ponder over many questions about life as you go back to yourself mentally and emotionally. This is because through practicing it you will find that the path to financial prosperity as well as personal growth becomes not only apparent but actually has meaning.

Self-Reflection Through Journaling

As such, writing in a journal for self-reflective purposes resembles viewing your inner being by means of a window. It's a technique used for deep thinking as well as clearing of minds, letting out the emotions and the growth in terms of the psyche state.

One can write in a simple mode on different pages of a journal about one's thoughts, emotions and experience. It is an opportunity to get to know yourself more deeply; express sides of your personality that otherwise couldn't be shown, and discover your true identity in all its dimensions.

Journaling goes beyond writing down daily happenings and having a diary. It is about talking to oneself, really speaking with itself. Journaling serves the purpose of unearthing those depths of an awareness, which exist in your thought. It is an outlet to express yourself in a safe environment where others understand your deepest fears and concerns without judgment.

Journal writing is imperative to self discovery. Externalizing the internal helps you analyze, understand, and reflect on writing down your thoughts or emotions. This is a kind of intercourse with yourself, a dialog which reveals our true beliefs, anxieties, and needs.

Keeping a journal helps to realize what hidden thoughts or attitudes lurk within them at the deepest level of their inner self.

This is also a place where you get to think about the most important events that made up your life, as well as find more details regarding the intricacies of your own personality. By keeping a journal, you can confront your inner demons, recognize your wins, and create objectives for yourself.

Remember just one workday, which was really busy. Upon getting home you pull out your diary and jot down everything that happened. Through that, you discover that the reason behind your stress is the more fundamental fear of failure and not simply your workload. The revelation leads you to examine yourself and your early life situation that subsequently improves your understanding of stress.

Let us imagine that you have to make a hard decision touching your private sphere. In the place of seeking counsel from other people; you refer to the journal. It is then that you realize what your gut tells by writing everything down in terms of pros and cons and then lead you to the most appropriate selection for oneself. This self-reflection exercise enables you to make a decision aligning with your genuine wishes.

Journaling may be one of the most significant activities that one will do in their lives. That will suffice, all that one needs is a notebook and pen for notes. Go to a quiet place where you can be alone and think through. Start by narrating your own day, events, emotions, and aspirations, at the very top of your writing. Do not be bound by any rigid structures, but allow your creativity flow freely.

You may write it down as you go through your experiences, making it a habit that happens every night or as a morning exercise that sets goals for the day. The bedroom should be able to serve like a canvas for your goals and dreams, a sanctuary for your toughest thoughts, and an office where difficult circumstances are processed. It is one way of expressing emotions, awareness, as well as growth as an individual.

Once you start doing this, discover how reflective the act of scribbling is and can bring a degree of therapeutic relief.

It turns into a reliable confidante, a mirror of your inner self, and a compass that points the way toward your personal growth and empowerment.

Mindfulness Meditation

You will need to do a profound thing like mindfulness meditation for you to understand yourself deeply so that such knowledge can help you in pursuing success.

It means that you should be aware of what is happening right now, accept your inner voice or thoughts without prejudice. Adopting this practice in your day-to-day activities could transform your entire existence. It will lead you to inner peace, emotional intelligence, and reveal the layers of self discovery that are all important in making money.

The mindful meditation technique entails focusing all your attention on what is happening, now. It is noting what is being experienced without biased mindfulness, not shutting off emotions. Awareness of how your mind works and what you think about will make it possible for you to have an understanding of yourself as who you really are at a deeper level. Increased self-awareness has proved itself as a great means of success in financial aspects.

Therefore, mindfulness meditation is important for self-discovery since it creates awareness of self. It allows you to probe into the intricacies of your emotions, thoughts, and bodily sensations. Through constant practice, you can excavate entrenched convictions, understand your drives, and spot trends in thought and feeling reactions. Making wise financial decisions requires being self-aware.

For example, let's say you are caught up in an argument with your peer at work. It prompts you or makes it imperative for you at a certain instant to observe your thoughts or feelings and not act out of impulse. Eventually, you could realize that the anger or frustration you experience towards certain people stems out from the deep-rooted fear of not being appreciated or understood.

This revelation can act as a powerful driving force for individual growth and self discovery.

It will also help you overcome obstacles at work more skillfully, which is essential for achieving financial success.

Think of it as a stressful day in the office, when anxiety is increasing.

This is where mindfulness meditation comes in and becomes your ultimate weapon against the control of these emotions.

It will give you an opportunity to set aside some time, whereby you shall sit still, and with a clear state of mind; focus on your breath in order to create the state of clarity and tranquility. This quiet will allow you to look at a way into which your stress falls into your order of priorities and values as well as its root causes. This will help you make wise financial decisions because it will see that your choices are connected to your specific and definite financial goals.

You don't have to go through a solitary retreat in some isolated monastery to embrace mindfulness meditation in your daily life. Concretely, it may simply involve sitting for five minutes every day and keeping quiet while reflecting. Find a quiet place where you can sit comfortably and clear your mind by focusing on the flow of air.

During meditation, you may at times have thoughts and feelings. Welcome them and make them feel welcome rather than pushing them away. Watching will just be like the curious scientist trying to understand his/her mind. This exercise can be done at the beginning of the day to take a jump start to the day on the right foot, at the breaks in between to keep focus, and after the close to let loose and take time to think about the day.

Seek Solitude

Make time in your life to spend alone. Spend some time alone in silent reflection and unplug from the incessant din of outside influences. A closer relationship with your inner self and time for introspection can be achieved through solitude. Taking time alone is like giving yourself a chance to really know who you are. In our busy lives, we get caught up in what others think and all the noise around us. But when you spend time alone, you create a quiet space to think about yourself without outside opinions.

Being alone helps you look inside and understand your thoughts and feelings better. It's like digging into your own mind to discover things about yourself that you might have forgotten or never paid attention to. This process of finding your true self happens slowly, like peeling off layers until you get to the real you.

Being by yourself also lets you grow as a person. You can face your fears, accept your weaknesses, and appreciate your strengths. Without others telling you what's right or wrong, you can embrace who you truly are and be okay with it.

When you make alone time a regular thing, you build a strong connection with your real self. This connection becomes like a guide, helping you make choices that match your values and dreams. It gives you the power to handle life's ups and downs while staying true to yourself.

Challenge Your Opinions

Put your life's worth of beliefs and convictions to the test. Do they really belong to you, or did outside forces mold them? You can discover what truly speaks to your true self by challenging and reevaluating your beliefs. Questioning your own beliefs is like giving them a friendly check-up, making sure they truly belong to you and not just something you picked up from others. It's a bit like cleaning out your mental closet, making sure all the ideas in there are ones you really believe in.

Imagine your beliefs are like clothes you wear in the world of ideas. Sometimes, we wear things just because everyone else is wearing them. Challenging your opinions is like taking a close look at each piece of clothing and asking, "Do I really like this, or am I wearing it because others are?"

This process is a journey into understanding what you genuinely believe. It's like peeling off layers of stickers that others might have stuck onto you. By questioning, you get to the core of your beliefs and discover if they resonate with your true self.

Think of it as cleaning the windows of your mind. When you challenge your opinions, it's like wiping away the dirt to see clearly. You might find some beliefs are there because your family or friends had them, not necessarily because they fit you. It's about making your beliefs your own, like choosing the decorations in your room to reflect your personality.

This self-discovery journey also allows room for growth. As you question and reevaluate, you might find new beliefs that better match who you are now. It's not about throwing away everything you thought before but refining and upgrading your mental wardrobe.

Explore Your Passions

Take part in things that actually make you happy and fulfilled. Discovering who you truly are is like a journey. It usually starts with looking at your interests. Doing things that truly make you happy and complete can be a strong way to find your real self. When you spend a lot of time doing things you like, like art or sports or hobbies, you find out what you really prefer in a better way.

Passions are like mirrors that show what you really want and care about inside you. They show a view of your basic self beyond what society expects or outward force. Consider the easy pleasure that comes when you are busy with a picture, hitting a goal or doing crafts - these times show parts of who you really are.

Art projects, like drawing or writing, let you show your feelings and ideas. By being creative, you touch feelings inside you. This helps you discover more about yourself. It might wake up parts of your personality that were sleeping. Likewise, sports and activities help you to get close to your body. This creates a friendly relationship between the brain and the body.

Having hobbies, such as gardening, cooking or playing an instrument can help us know more about ourselves. They let you try out your skills, find hidden skills, and build a feeling of control. In these times of getting involved, you might discover small hints about what really connects with your deep inner self.

By always taking part in things that make you happy, you learn more about what you really like. This continuing search slowly shows who you really are, and helps you see the difference between what others want from you and what you truly want. It's not about how hard your dreams are but the honest way you take them on.

Embrace Vulnerability

Letting yourself be open and admit weakness is a strong way to show your real self. It helps you find out more about who you are deeply inside. This means telling your deepest thoughts and feelings to people you can trust, such as a therapist or close friends. This doesn't have to be for everybody but just these special ones that we know will listen carefully. This act of showing weakness makes it possible for true self-knowledge and deep feelings to happen.

When you let yourself be open, true sincerity comes into your connections. Telling others about your fears, big hopes and worries helps make stronger bonds with the people near you. This way of being open makes a place where you feel safe and understood. It helps you find parts of yourself that were kept secret or pushed away before.

In a safe place like the office of a therapist or with close friends, showing our feelings can lead to self-knowledge. This makes us understand ourselves better. Talking about your feelings lets you look at them better. It helps make clear what emotions are most important to you. With this step, you learn more about what makes you move forward. Fears and wants come out too. This helps to give a full view of who is really in the deep part that's not always seen from outside.

Moreover, being vulnerable helps us to grow emotionally. When you tell others about your problems, it helps you understand and deal with feelings. This makes your spirit stronger and gives a sense of self that's not shaken by setbacks or hard times. These shared experiences help you learn to accept your flaws and see that being open is not a sign of shame but leads to courage.

By sharing what you're feeling inside with others, it gives them a chance to do the same back. This back-and-forth sharing strengthens bonds and offers different looks at your own happenings. It's a two-way sharing that leads to joint learning and understanding. This boosts the self-discovery process.

Analyze Your Principles

Determine your basic beliefs by taking some time. Which values and principles are most important to you? Living authentically requires that you live in accordance with your values. Looking at and getting a handle on your beliefs is a basic action to discover the parts of your real self. It means you take time to think and find out the main ideas that lead your life. These things show the way, guiding you to be real and live a life that matches your deepest beliefs.

Think of this as a trip to find what's most important to you. Your beliefs are like a guide, affecting what you choose and do. Take a moment to think about what really touches your heart and soul. This thinking doesn't need big fancy ideas but just understanding what feels good and important for you.

Finding out your beliefs is like finding the parts you need to make your life strong. These can go from being truthful and nice to stick-to-itiveness and feeling for others. By knowing these basic rules, you make a life true to yourself. Living that way means matching what you do with these rules. It's about including your beliefs in your daily decisions, big and small.

When your actions match your beliefs, there's a feeling of inner harmony. This match is important for finding the real you because it shows that what you say you believe matches how you actually live. Ideas work like a good guide, helping to make decisions in life. When you have to make choices or solve problems, thinking about your beliefs can show you the way. This understanding comes from knowing what's really important to you. It helps you make decisions that match your true self.

Listen To Your Inner Voice

Discovering your true self involves connecting with your inner voice and intuition. This internal guide, often drowned out by daily noise, helps you understand your real desires and feelings.

Your inner voice is a gentle guide, sharing insights that may get lost in the busyness of life. To access this authenticity, practice mindfulness. Take a moment in your day's quiet spaces to listen with an open heart, not just your ears.

Our bodies, messengers of truth, play a crucial role. Notice how your body reacts – tension, lightness, warmth. These physical cues express your genuine reactions in the journey of self-discovery.

Imagine making a decision. Instead of relying only on logic, turn inward. Listen to your intuition's soft murmurs. It's not about complex analysis but recognizing quiet wisdom. This is your true self's language, and understanding it requires being present.

Authentic decisions come from the blend of inner guidance and bodily wisdom. Trust your instincts, embrace what feels right. It's not about grand words; it's about embracing the simplicity of your inner truths.

Self-discovery is a journey of self-listening, where your genuine self's whispers guide you. The path isn't adorned with big words; it's paved with sincerity and a true connection to your innermost self. In your inner world's quiet, find the courage to unlock your true self, one authentic decision at a time.

Learn From Life Experiences

Reflecting on your life experiences, both challenging and rewarding, serves as a method for unlocking the door to your true self. Life is a series of lessons, and within these moments of difficulty and triumph lie valuable insights about your personality and inner self.

Think of your life as a story, with each experience contributing a chapter to your personal narrative. Difficult times often act as mirrors, reflecting aspects of yourself that may go unnoticed during smoother periods. By examining your reactions to challenges, you gain a deeper understanding of your strengths, resilience, and coping mechanisms.

Consider moments of failure not as setbacks but as opportunities for self-discovery. How you respond to adversity reveals your character and provides clues about your values. It's in these tough times that you can uncover hidden strengths, resilience, and even areas for personal growth. Embracing these lessons from challenges can be a transformative journey toward understanding your true self.

On the flip side, moments of achievement also offer insights. Your reactions to success unveil aspects of your aspirations, values, and sources of fulfillment. What brings you joy and satisfaction in moments of triumph can guide you towards activities and pursuits that align with your authentic self.

Life experiences are like a mosaic, composed of various pieces that together create a picture of who you are. Each interaction, whether positive or negative, contributes to the intricate design of your personality. By taking the time to reflect on these experiences, you piece together a clearer understanding of your preferences, passions, and reactions.

Adorn Yourself With Genuineness

Being yourself and exploring who you are isn't just about thinking—it's also about having real support. Picture your life like a woven blanket, made of connections and relationships. When you weave these threads with people who value and accept your real self, you create a caring environment for self-discovery.

Think about how relationships affect finding your true self. When you connect with people who appreciate your realness, you feel accepted and belong. In this mutual understanding, judgment fades away, letting your true self unfold.

These connections act like mirrors, showing you who you are. With accepting people, you feel seen and heard, creating a safe space for self-exploration. It's like being in a garden where each flower represents a part of your personality, and these genuine connections help your true self grow.

Simplicity is key in these relationships. It's not about big gestures or fancy talks but sharing real moments. Laughter, shared experiences, and understanding glances create a supportive backdrop for self-discovery.

Imagine talking freely without fearing judgment. These interactions let you express yourself, a safe space to uncover layers of your true self. The simplicity of acceptance in these relationships guides you to understand who you are.

As you surround yourself with these genuine connections, you see that self-discovery isn't a lonely journey but a group effort. Being valued for who you are creates an atmosphere where your true self can comfortably emerge, like a flower enjoying the warmth of understanding. In these relationships, you discover the beauty and strength in being appreciated for your real self.

Challenge Your Comfort Zone

Finding your true self is like going on an exciting journey, and a great guide for this trip is stepping out of what feels familiar. Think of your comfort zone as a cozy bubble where everything is known and safe. Going beyond it is like sailing into unknown waters, where you can discover hidden parts of yourself.

Challenging your comfort zone would be like packing a bag and going to a big city. The new sights, sounds, and even different foods open doors to parts of yourself that might have been quiet. It's not about doing something extreme; it's about gently pushing what feels safe.

Trying new things is like reading a book you've never read before. Each part reveals something new about your story. Maybe it's trying different food, learning a new skill, or doing activities you've never thought about. These simple steps outside your usual routine can be like opening windows to freshen up your life.

Obstacles, unexpected challenges, are like puzzles waiting to be solved. Facing challenges taps into your inner strength and creativity. This is about handling the ups and downs of life. Each success, no matter how small, adds to your self-discovery.

The beauty of this method is in its simplicity. It doesn't need big actions; it just asks you to stretch yourself a bit. Picture a butterfly coming out of its cocoon; challenging your comfort zone is like spreading your wings and realizing your own potential.

In the simplicity of pushing boundaries, you find a playground for self-exploration. It's like finding new colors on a palette you never knew existed. Venturing beyond your comfort zone might lead you to discover preferences and passions you never knew you had. In these moments of exploration, your true self, like a hidden treasure, starts to show itself, piece by simple piece.

Embrace Imperfection

Discovering your true self becomes easier when you fully accept imperfections. Picture a world where chasing perfection is like chasing something you can never catch. Knowing that perfection is a myth helps you explore yourself in a simple yet deep way.

Think of imperfections as unique strokes on your individual canvas. Each flaw adds to the masterpiece that is you. It's like a mosaic where the broken pieces make a pattern that's uniquely yours. Embracing these imperfections is not about settling; it's about seeing the beauty in your genuine, unfiltered self.

Imagine a field of daisies. No two are exactly the same, but each one shows the beauty of being itself. Accepting imperfections is like recognizing the beauty that comes from being authentic. It's not about fitting an ideal image; it's about becoming the fullest version of your true self.

Picture a world without the pressure to be flawless, where mistakes are not failures but chances to learn. Embracing imperfection is like giving yourself permission to be human, to grow from experiences instead of being held back by an impossible standard. Your worth isn't tied to a perfect image but to your genuine, imperfect essence.

This method is simple because it's something everyone can relate to. Imperfections are part of being human, connecting us in our uniqueness. When you accept your imperfections, you open a door to loving and accepting yourself. It's like saying, "This is me, flaws and all," and finding strength in that honesty.

Discovering your true self means letting go of societal expectations and perfectionist ideas. It's about proudly owning your imperfections and realizing they're not obstacles but paths to self-discovery. Like a tree with twisted branches, your imperfections tell a story of resilience, growth, and authenticity. Embracing imperfection uncovers the raw beauty of your true self, perfectly imperfect in every way.

Connect With Nature

Get away from the bustle of modern life and spend time in nature. We can find our true essence and sense of grounding in nature. Self-discovery can be sparked by the natural world's simplicity and beauty.

This allows you to engage in a personal, yet deep journey of self-discovering. In essence, your inner landscape will come to a revelation. As this happens, you will find out that both personal growth and monetary success stem from your actual self, which has been well-hidden from view.

Life recognition is hard to exaggerate as it means knowing who you are as an individual. Such makes it the pillar of purposeful, authentic, and gratifying life. Knowing yourself enables you to have a logical understanding of your own values, objectives, and interests.

This self-awareness acts as a compass for your decision making regarding finances.

Connecting to your true self will allow you to have control over your finances, which should align with your vision for the future. The real needs start becoming reflected in the way you handle your finances, career and lifestyle. Pursuing financial opportunities that you really look forward to will motivate you, satisfy you and cause you to succeed.

The process of finding your authentic self will be a lifetime journey involving constant reflection, education, and growth. Treat it like a step into personal power and transformation. You will know the true self and this is your true wealth, a well of possible happiness.

The Power Of Self-Acceptance

One important but frequently disregarded cornerstone of personal development is self-acceptance. It's the act of accepting and valuing who you really are—flaws and all—without holding yourself to any standards or passing judgment. This idea is about accepting your intrinsic value as a special individual, not about becoming complacent.

Being at peace with oneself is a profound state of being known as self-acceptance. It means realizing that your past experiences, flaws, or mistakes do not define who you are. It's about letting go of self-doubt and self-criticism so that you can grow and change without having to carry the weight of self-criticism.

Picture yourself at a family reunion where everyone is sharing their accomplishments, milestones, and seemingly perfect lives. Your cousin just got a promotion, your sister is about to finish her master's degree, and your best friend recently got engaged.

Even with all the celebrations, you can't help but feel inadequate and self-conscious. You begin to wonder why you haven't reached comparable milestones and begin to doubt your own journey.

Many people have had experiences similar to this one. This is a scenario where feelings of unworthiness can arise from a lack of self-acceptance. You might make the mistake of evaluating your value by outside norms and comparing yourself to others rather than appreciating your own journey and achievements.

Let's now investigate how self-acceptance can change this situation.

Imagine yourself at the same family get-together, but with a profound sense of acceptance of who you are. You now know how to accept your path, your accomplishments, and your failures. You truly rejoice in your cousin's success when they tell you about their promotion because you know it doesn't take away from your own value or path. You recognize that your path is distinct and that your timeline is your own, which is why you are pleased with your sister's academic achievement and your friend's engagement.

In this case, self-acceptance enables you to live in the present and truly celebrate your loved ones' successes and happiness. You are also released from the weight of insecurity and comparison. You now gauge your value based on your own sense of fulfillment and authenticity rather than on the opinions of others.

Being self-accepting does not entail being lazy or uninspired. It's about loving yourself through life's highs and lows and realizing your intrinsic worth. It entails realizing that no one path leads to success or personal development and that your journey is distinct. You have strengths and weaknesses, victories and setbacks, just like everyone else. You can accept these parts of yourself without passing judgment when you have self-acceptance.

Practically speaking, there are a number of ways to foster self-acceptance. For instance, self-compassion can help you replace self-critical thoughts with self-awareness through mindfulness meditation. By exploring your thoughts and feelings in a journal, you can get insight into how you see yourself.

By practicing self-care, you reaffirm that you are deserving of love and attention. A supportive environment that fosters authenticity and is conducive to self-acceptance can be created by surrounding oneself with positive people.

It is easier to understand that self-improvement is a journey rather than a destination when you set reasonable goals for your own development as opposed to aiming for perfection. The cornerstone of an authentic and fulfilling life is self-acceptance. You can handle the ups and downs with grace and resiliency thanks to it. You can discover true contentment and a closer bond with others and yourself by valuing your journey and embracing your uniqueness.

Treating yourself with the same consideration and compassion that you would give to a friend going through a difficult time is the essence of self-compassion. It's critical to understand that everyone makes mistakes and that these setbacks or mistakes don't define who you are.

As a tool for self-acceptance, self-compassion entails accepting your humanity and acting with kindness and understanding, just as you would for a close friend or family member. By gradually changing your self-talk from self-criticism to self-kindness, this practice has the potential to be transformative.

Beyond financial success, emotional health is improved by self-acceptance. It's essential for building resilience, lowering stress levels, and accepting uncomfortable feelings without passing judgment. Your relationships are affected because you make genuine connections and have rewarding, candid, and transparent conversations.

In the end, self-acceptance results in a happy and purposeful life. It's about living a genuine life and making decisions that align with your values and actual desires. It is the cornerstone of a well-lived life, in which contentment and happiness are just as important as material wealth in determining success.

Embracing Change: The Secret to Your Own Personal Revolution

Change is a force of nature, an ever-present aspect of our lives. It's often perceived as a disruptor, something that throws us off balance, but in reality, it's the very essence of growth and personal transformation.

In this chapter, I'll take you through the vital role that embracing change plays in your journey towards becoming the best version of yourself.

Change signifies progress. It opens new doors, provides fresh perspectives, and invites opportunities for self-improvement. When we resist change, we resist the chance to evolve, adapt, and thrive.

Now, it's natural to feel apprehensive about change. The unknown can be intimidating. We often cling to our comfort zones, resisting anything that challenges our routines. However, true growth can only occur when we step outside of these boundaries.

So, how can you fully embrace change for personal transformation? Start by shifting your perspective. Understand that change is inevitable and, most importantly, that it's a catalyst for self-improvement.

Think about the metamorphosis of a caterpillar into a butterfly. It doesn't resist the change from a crawling creature to a creature that can soar. Rather, it gives in to the process, allowing itself to be dismantled and then rebuilt into something lovely and liberated.

In a similar vein, accepting personal change necessitates giving in to the transformational process of oneself.

What can you do when it comes to accepting change? Make it your starting point by embracing a growth mentality.

Besides creating strategies for self-growth, developing a financially conscious mentality that thrives amidst defeat, resilience, and never-ending progress are also vital for wealth creation.

Most beginners suffer from insecurity and lack sufficient funding.

These challenges are an opportunity to grow and should be viewed as obstacles that need to be tackled rather than insipid obstructions. Every financial problem will provide a chance for you to improve on your money management skills.
Accept the fact that challenges and failures provide opportunities for growth. Look at them as ways of making a better you, not obstacles.

One should also learn to embrace new experiences in order to cope with change. Investing novices might have entered unknown waters in such areas as investment, budgeting and credit management. As such, they become ready to explore unknown waters by embracing change and having an appetite for new experiences. Instead of trying everything at once, beginners can welcome change in order to try out a lot of financial opportunities and get familiar with different strategies in order to increase their chances of finding something that works well for them.

Change acceptance lets new entrants try alternative financing opportunities and techniques that they feel might be fit for their business.
You should also look for opportunities to move out of your comfort zone. Visit different areas, do various activities, and interact with people from every walk of life. Doing this will make you perceive things differently and give you a fresh outlook on life.

Besides, learn how to detach from the old world. They only make you feel heavy with any regrets, grudges that used to happen in the course of time, some mistakes committed. Such a perspective may set you liberated as you move toward a better life. A number of novices have regrets or are carrying around previous money mistakes.

They may have missed an opportunity, mismanaged money, or otherwise acted in ways they regret. With regard to this, being ready for change assumes the idea that your financial destiny does not depend on your previous behavior. A new opportunity for making better choices comes everyday.

Another aspect to accepting change is realizing life is not a straight corridor or linear path.
Successful financial path is not a straight path.
In fact, it is very common for you, especially being a newbie, to experience both lows and highs, losses not justified by initial investment or just lack of money.

Change acceptance entails understanding that success within the business can never be immediate. The road is filled with dangers. There are some disappointments here and there. Setbacks should not be seen as barriers to overcome but instead they form the building blocks to success.

Also, be sure that the people around are supporting and uplifting your transformation.
This would go a long way in advising novices on the appropriate financial advice.
Change acceptance implies a readiness to consult senior colleagues in order to get advice or mentoring. Achieving financial success usually translates to understanding what others have done,

learning from their experiences, then coming up with ideas that will work for you.

New investors need to find mentors, friends or role models that can guide and motivate them.

Build up a support system that is composed of advisers, mentors, friends, and well-wishers with whom you can share ideas and who will acknowledge all your achievements—big or small.

Despite all of us wanting to be rich, it is not always an easy way for everyone.
However, it is full of detours, obstacles and uncertainties particularly for the beginners.
The following shows the impact of "embracing change" in terms of suffering from early loss and subsequent prosperity.

Introducing Sara, a college graduate brimming with dreams and ambitions. She was determined to conquer the financial world. She landed a decent job, made a budget, and even invested in some stocks she thought were promising.
But as the months went by, Sara faced a cruel reality. Her investments tanked, and she found herself

barely making ends meet. It was a time of crippling self-doubt and regret. She felt that perhaps she didn't have what it took to navigate the world of finance.

Jake is the protagonist of this tale; he is an ambitious businessman who launched his own website. He was incredibly optimistic and thought his business would succeed beyond belief.

However, as the months stretched into years, Jake came to understand that there was much more work involved in becoming a successful entrepreneur. He faced obstacles related to money, erratic earnings, and the threat of bankruptcy.

Almost out of their minds, Sara and Jake wondered about their financial endeavors and the decisions they had made. They were left with two choices: give up on their goals or welcome change. Thankfully, they made the latter decision.

Sara came to realize that achieving financial success required knowledge of and flexibility in the constantly changing financial landscape.
Rather than giving up, she threw herself into self-education. She kept an eye on the markets, studied financial books, and gained knowledge from

her early investing blunders. She realized the value of having a growth mindset and realized that she needed to view her financial difficulties as chances for personal development.

She diversified her investments, consulted financial mentors, and developed a newfound resolve as she started to view the market's volatility as a platform for creativity.
Her portfolio grew and her ability to withstand financial setbacks increased with time. Sara had become a wise financial person after rising from the ashes of her first failure.

Jake's journey as an entrepreneur was equally difficult. Rather than running from the uncertainty and anxiety, he made the choice to adjust and welcome the constantly shifting online business environment.
He turned his energies toward solving problems and let go of his regrets from the past.

Jake came to see that every challenge he faced presented an opportunity for creativity and advancement.

He put various strategies into practice, gained knowledge from both his triumphs and setbacks, and started to view the wild ride, that is, entrepreneurship as a necessary component of the game. With renewed determination and self-control, his business began to take off. Jake had changed not just his company but also himself. He came out as a successful businessman who had welcomed change.

In Sara and Jake's experiences, the power of "embracing change" was evident. They discovered that early setbacks in the financial sector presented chances for development and transformation rather than being judgments of ineptitude. This viewpoint created opportunities for learning, flexibility, and creativity.

Living examples of the transformative nature of the road to financial success, as demonstrated by Sara and Jake, were resilience, adaptability, and an unwavering belief in one's own abilities.
The experiences of Sara and Jake provide a priceless lesson for all newcomers aiming for financial success: although the path to wealth may be fraught with challenges, by accepting change, those same

challenges can be transformed into stepping stones leading to success.

To put it simply, accepting change means realizing that it is inevitable and that it can lead to advancement and personal development. It's an invitation to let go of control, venture outside of your comfort zone, and cultivate a growth mindset in the process of transformation. Although the path won't always be easy, accepting change is a decision you make to grow, adjust, and prosper.

Identifying and Breaking Limiting Beliefs

One powerful enemy that frequently lurks in the background when it comes to both financial success and personal development is limiting beliefs. These walls we put up for ourselves can act as imperceptible chains that hold us back and keep us from realizing our greatest potential.
But as we go through life and explore the complex realm of self-improvement, recognizing and

dispelling these limiting ideas turns into a crucial first step on the path to personal development.

The reason is that these beliefs act as unconscious saboteurs in the backs of numerous people. However, they significantly affect us and our chances to become successful.

We must first acknowledge these limiting beliefs for what they are: embedded beliefs which hamper our financial pursuits and block growth and development until they are addressed.

Such limiting beliefs are often a product of external factors, social upbringing, and previous occurrences. The creeping, silent fears which have snuck into our lives day by day include, "I am bad about finances", "I can never make it" or " I am not good about investments". These thoughts lodge themselves deep in our subconscious and govern every word we utter and action we take.

A process of self exploration becomes necessary for an individual to see and address these beliefs. We've seen before that it starts with meditation and self-reflection. This will enable us to dig out the self limiting beliefs by just considering our thoughts and emotions. These might manifest themselves as negative talk about the self, the fear of taking a risk financially, or the conviction that success belongs to other people.

Challenging the common beliefs is a step towards breaking the limiting beliefs.

It necessitates contemplation and introspection. First is, wonder about where these beliefs originated. Have these been beliefs that have stayed with you or do they stem from facts and experience? On multiple occasions, we discover that most of our restricting assumptions are simply based on mere perception without any solid evidence to back them up.

The voice of our limiting beliefs shows its face as negative self-talk. It is that nagging voice in your mind that asks questions and generates fear. Awareness is very crucial, especially when these dehumanizing phrases or ideas will be mentioned.

Face them with self-talk that is uplifting and full of affirmations. Recognize that you are not an exception and that everyone has the ability to develop and succeed.

Knowledge about what should not be accepted in life is a vital aspect of the journey towards awareness and self-improvement. It is a mental process with its own perception.

Demolish such beliefs; then begin to incorporate optimistic thoughts and beliefs that uphold your financial goals.

What makes discovering and overcoming limiting beliefs so important on the path of becoming wealthy? These beliefs have a remarkable impact on our financial decisions.

These may lead into one having doubts or doing nothing whenever such chances are presented upon them.

It can pose a huge barrier to your efforts of creating some budget if you have this limiting belief that you are not capable of handling money. Your conviction that you cannot ever become rich might discourage you from investing opportunities that can make you richer.

Overcoming these barriers opens up opportunities to make your own financial decisions. It prompts prudent investments, careful risks, and confidently snatching up the chances in time. Stop letting the fear, doubt, and self-limiting beliefs hold you back so that you can enhance your odds in becoming financially successful.

The Role of Empathy in Personal Development

One of those strong influences which are mostly ignored, yet highly effective in people's development. Empathy does not apply in interpersonal relationships and social interactions alone but is important in our growth processes towards self-financing.

Empathy can be defined as an ability to understand and even feel another's emotions or sentiments. It refers to being able to put yourself in someone else's shoes, to share their feelings and offer genuine support and understanding.

It is closely connected to the way in which we relate with others; however, its effects extend beyond this as it affects our self-concept and development as individuals.

To be empathic, start with self-empathy at home. This implies self-awareness, understanding one's feelings and emotions and treating oneself like a dear friend. Self-empathy helps you appreciate individualism, love yourself and your flaws, as well as forgive oneself.

Personal growth requires self acceptance and it starts with self-empathy. It is a pillar used in building your resilience and empathy. Promoting self-awareness, self-empathy allows one to uncover one's ground values and aim.

By growing in self-empathy, there is a tendency of becoming more sympathetic in your relationships with other people.

Empathy serves for an establishment of deep and serious relationships. Empathy is an essential tool of personal growth, learning, and understanding during one's life journey.

What is the connection between being financially successful and experiencing empathy? This is all about understanding how financial decisions work and what impact it has on you and other people's lives.

Consider financial planning and investment. By taking up an empathetic stance, one can also determine investment returns as well as ethical/social impacts. One can consider investing in ventures that make you rich and give towards such organizations in consonance with one's principles.

Empathy also applies in the financial talks and negotiations. It is possible to arrive at a cooperative solution if one party understands the needs and views of the other parties. It may lead to creation of empathetic allies, partnerships, deals, and even relationships with a possibility of being based on empathy and not just rivalry and competitions.

To realize empathy for successful growth and profit, you should improve your understanding of and relating to people on a higher level. It's all about understanding that sympathy is a powerful instrument to progress and not a handicap.

Remember that empathy goes together with challenges of individual progress toward riches. Start with the practice of self-compassion, remain open to understanding how others think, and employ empathy as you make money related choices.

Having this capability will make you feel successful on a personal and economic level, providing your happiness with greater depth.
Empathy is an important thread running through, boosting understanding, and driving both your financial and personal growth.

Chapter 2

Setting Your Life Goals

At the heart of personal growth and financial success lies a simple yet transformative concept: goal setting. It is the thread which unites wishes and makes them come true revealing to us the road towards a bright and rich future.

In essence, goal setting is making a map of one's life. The process of imagining a desired future for yourself is accompanied with formulating feasible steps towards realizing those dreams. The goals serve as a guide, directing us forward, and they provide the inspiration for our efforts. They link the point of departure and the target destination.

Goal setting is not confined to wish fulfillment. It entails outlining details, accuracy, and taking steps to actualize desires. This is making a choice on where you are going, how do you intend to get there and at what time?

Goal setting is very vital and important. Setting goals makes life meaningful and gives its shape. These are navigational instruments that enhance our concentration leading productivity and reducing chances of procrastination. In simple terms, these guideposts direct our way through the wide ocean of life.

Setting a goal means you are simply choosing what objective you desire for in the future. By simply making the commitment to yourself, you make a vow to be responsible for it. Through goals, you take charge of time, relieve yourself of stress, and sharpen your focus.

Specificity is the initial step in defining objectives. Your mind becomes more involved in the pursuit of your goals when they are specifically defined.

Specificity adds an air of reality to your dreams, so they become more achievable.

Just as you paint a vivid picture of your upcoming future by setting specific goals. This gives you an opportunity to picture how your future shall be after success is attained. Your energy source is your vision that makes you act.

Layering your aspirations begins with defining your goals. It lends meaning to your life and increases your confidence.

In defining your aims, you are basically indicating what success means to you. The simple fact of putting these aspirations onto paper is transforming; it brings them to life, gives them concrete form and adds emotional value through the act of writing. Verbalizing your goals brings about a commitment towards yourself.

They enter your mind, influencing what you think and do. Each of your obstacles becomes an opportunity whereby you are ready to challenge yourself.

Your goals will be unachievable, unless they can be measured. Thus it implies that you should define parameters for checking whether you are on course or not. Goal without measurement is like a ship without a compass; it has no directionality or urgency. Setting standards for achieving your goals helps inspire you and hold you up to yourself.

Moreover, it lets you see what position you are in and enables you to record your improvement. While this measure motivates you towards your destination.

However it takes courage and responsibility to achieve goals. All of you should take charge of your trip. This path is not always easy; it's here that commitment comes in handy.

Achieving steadfastness necessitates accountability as well as a means of growth. Commitment can be demonstrated in several ways such as being personally responsible, attending weekly meetings or the power of an accountability partner to make sure you do not stay behind.

Following this, a focus will be made on reducing the purpose to a series of manageable activities. The little objectives will make the larger targets seem less daunting. Its time management skills improve productivity while boosting concentration.

It's all about being comfortable living. Nevertheless, one needs to choose suitable halts to reach there. Prioritizing this way ensures that the limited time and energy are appropriately put into the right places. This puts more emphasis on good qualities such as proper time management, keenness, reduced level of anxiousness, among others. Concentrating on attaining some of the goals out of your objectives is the best way you can meet them. Priority enables you to focus on only what is important, thus short-cutting your way towards your goals.

Lifelong goals determine what people do to lead them to developing their abilities, maintaining effective relations with others, earning money, and taking care of health. These objectives will be your driving force to seek a better and purposeful life. That makes your person who you envisage him becoming. The trip consists of huge dreams and little deeds that constitute achievements along the way. That is, having a vision in mind of what you want to see happening and for the purposes be set right.

However, the secret to achieving such dreams is to begin with goal setting.

Here, this indicates the specificity of definitions which are directed towards your concentration as well as a focus on accomplishment. They make goals like a lighthouse amid the storms of life. Significant targets, measurable metrics, and also timelines enable you to do something, but at the same time control your pulse. Your goals become more.

Creating a Vision Board for Your Life

Making a personal vision board on the dream-come-true trip for your life in a nutshell. This is a very potent visual approach of charting one's ambitions, goals, and the innermost needs. This apparently simple thing but yet tremendously life changing, is able to change fates and release latent capacities.

Think of a blank canvas with you being the painter with your dreams and aspirations as the varied hues. This canvas is a vision board where you make a picture of your dream life.

A collage of pictures, words, and symbols representing your dream, no matter if it is associated with your professional affairs, relations with another person, a trip, health, etc. However, a vision board is way more than just a bunch of nice-looking images and serves as a path to your destiny.

The fascinating process utilizes the powers of the mind and the law of attraction. With meticulous selection of meaningful pictures, you tell yourself who you want to be, in a way that is crystal-clear to your unconsciousness. Hence, your mind starts working to connect your present life with the bright future that you are describing: "this is what I need" and "it is who I want to be".

Vision board, crafted properly, is not only an artistic work but even more, a live power of change. It acts as a constant reminder for your dreams to take action. This drives you a step further in your quest to move an inch ahead of yesterday; it also motivates you, influences your decisions, and gives you an acute concentration. This is similar to carrying a personal GPS in your lives' journey, guiding you toward the destinations that matter most.

However, a vision board works with much more than just its practical value. It is a strikingly beautiful portrayal of the power in all of us. It shows how strong dreams are, and how people can shape their destiny.

A vision for a better world, full of diversions and doubts can serve as a beam of light, an intention declared, and the confirmation of endless opportunities for those who will dream, picture, and take action.

The Power of Visualization

Clarity Of Goals

Visualization is the ultimate gift toward clarity when it comes to personal goals as far as finances are concerned. Success does not have any reference to dreamy hopes or unrealistic ideals. It is much more to the precision of creating a mental map guiding one to predetermined targets. When you close your eyes and visualize your goals like buying an imaginary house, starting one big company or hitting a $10,000 salary per month, you would be able to imagine those targets in very clear images.

The image will give you something to aim at because it is so sharp and clear. This is like giving coordinates for your navigation; it shows exactly how to transform mental images into reality. This helps you be more focused on goals setting and planning your strategy. You move along in a single thought aimed at achieving these goals indefatigably.

Mental Rehearsals

In the realm of financial success, visualization is like a dress rehearsal for life's grandest performance. Just as athletes mentally prepare for their competitions, engage in a mental rehearsal of your financial victories. Vividly simulate the process of achieving your goals, step by step.

This practice has profound effects on your confidence and competence. When you visualize yourself handling financial challenges with grace, it's like practicing your skills in a safe mental space. This not only boosts your self-assurance but also minimizes the anxiety that often accompanies new endeavors. You will find that when you eventually face real-world challenges, you will be better prepared because you have already tackled them in your mind.

Positive Mindset

Visualization is the architect of a positive mindset. It's more than just wishful thinking; it's about cultivating an unwavering belief in the possibility of success. When you visualize financial prosperity, you focus not only on the end results but on the emotions and sensations that accompany them.
You will feel the rush of accomplishment, the satisfaction of achieving your goals, and the tangible rewards that follow.

These positive feelings become a magnetic force, attracting opportunities and like-minded individuals who share your optimism. This optimistic outlook doesn't just influence your mental state; it also impacts your actions. Find yourself taking steps with confidence, enthusiasm, and a can-do attitude. It's a self-fulfilling prophecy where the positivity you have cultivated through visualization propels you to make choices and take actions that lead to financial success.

Decision Making

Visualization is not merely a passive exercise; it's an active tool that guides you in making well-informed decisions on your journey to financial success. When you visualize your goals and the path to achieve them, it's not just about daydreaming. It's a practical strategy to foresee the consequences of your choices.

I play out different scenarios in my mind, contemplating how each decision might affect my progress. This mental foresight is invaluable.

It allows me to make choices that align with my long-term financial vision, rather than being swayed by short-term temptations or concerns. It's like having a built-in decision-making advisor in my mind.

When faced with dilemmas or crossroads, I turn to the mental images I've created through visualization to seek guidance. This process ensures that my decisions are aligned with my ultimate financial goals.

Resilience

Obstacles are what you meet on the road to success. Thus, visualization comes in handy since it avails you with a particular kind of mental toughness and problem resolution. Then whenever you come across impediments or obstructions which one did not expect, then refer to the pictures of success you had drawn in your mind.

They are sources of inspiration and determination for that matter.

Creativity is critical in most financial success ventures. Visualize solutions for financial obstacles that may appear on your way. Visualize different possible scenarios and consequences in the mind's eye. In doing so, you will be able to consider various alternatives, predict problems, and refine your approaches.

By taking part in this mental experiment, it will help you think outside the box and overcome the financial barriers. You will mentally be running through possible problems with various solutions to see which would apply best.

The memories of my journey into financial success include the triumphant moments, waiting for the success, and the dreams I have imagined. They have a mental resilience, which ensures that they keep going on the same path. That's the inner voice that tells me no letdown should dishearten one, but instead, go on overcoming setbacks, learn lessons from failures and adapt strategies over challenges. An invaluable weapon against disheartening obstacles whose paths seem uncertain even during the most daunting journeys.

Networking And Relationships

However, visualization is not only done for your sole benefit, but also to help build relationships and networks. Once, the mind begins to conjure up images of fruitful engagements with congruent people that are willing to collaborate towards achieving financial success, then the journey will take shape. This is how you will get involved in real discussions, make important deals, and exploit your relations towards common development.

This is not just wishful thinking, but an active means of fostering business relationships. Have the attitude of an achiever when interacting with new and old friends. This positive attitude coupled with networking will see you make invaluable affiliations and mentorship as well as open up more possibilities which might have been unknown to you.

Inspiration For Action

Visualization is just one aspect of the activity which should be used to stimulate and support actions. Whenever you have pictures of having done well financially in your mind, they set fire inside you that makes it real after all. The pictures you will see will be what will inspire you when you are creating your mental images. Sooner, you'll be rushing forward to action in the pursuit of your objectives.

The images you have imagined constitute magnetism attracting you towards the conduct and practice that will realize your financial dreams. This serves as an inspiration for your ambition.

The purpose is to instigate persistent and concentrated action towards realizing objectives. In this context, visualization refers to what ignites the spirit of determination that enables one to advance from planning to action.

Defining SMART Financial Goals

For instance, SMART financial goals represent creating a road map to success.

It is a fascinating and inspiring process through which people get skills to transform their financial dreams into reality. SMART is not just mere guidelines; it is a revolutionary framework which clarifies, structures and makes accountability in your financial goals and objectives.

Visualize holding a perfectly calibrated compass that every single S-M-A-R-T letter corresponds with one of four directions on the route towards achieving your targets. However, specificity serves as your beacon, which leads you to express clearly what your financial desires are.

Being measurable implies having well-defined objectives and a set of clear criteria that you can use to assess your advancement, serving as your compass for determining your progression.

Achievability is what holds your dreams from becoming fantasies while making them realities. Importantly, relevance ensures that your monetary goals are aligned with your general outlooks on life, preventing you from being drifted away from getting rich. The time-bound here is the clock, telling you that each aspiration or objective has its deadline or limit; hence, it is always good to know what time is best for accomplishing a certain target.

When SMART is used effectively, each element forms a bedrock supporting financial prosperity. Having specific set goals also gives you clarity on where you want to be, whether in your retirement, paying off debts, or even the ownership of a house.
Goals that are measurable give you concrete aims that can be used to measure your progress, and therefore be celebrated as milestones towards achieving your objectives.

Achievable goals keep your dreams within grasp, fostering positive feelings like empowerment and avoiding self-defeat messages. Specifically, relevant goals link your financial objectives with the meaning of your life.

A time-sensitive goal pushes you toward steady efforts, so that you remain clear about the possibility of being overtaken by procrastination.

To help define smart objectives will elaborate further on each attribute of this powerful framework in this exploration of defining SMART financial objectives. It is my responsibility to reveal how to make your financial goals correspond with your particular values and provide real tactics to set up, measure and achieve your financial targets.

The journey is not merely a budgetary plan but a transformation experience by taking control of one's financial destiny stepwise where SMART goals materialize lifelong dreams into reality. Therefore, join me on this enchanting journey in setting up smart financial objectives that bridge with the normal realm and elevate you to the realm of dreamers.

Setting SMART financial targets translates to drawing a precise picture of where one's treasures lie. This framework is composed of four gems, all of which are very important for success; these are: Specific, Measurable, Achievable, and Relevant as well as Time-bound. The targets are not simply random figures and dates. They are meaningful messages that guide you through your financial pathway.

Your journey starts with specific goals. They want you to tell them exactly what your goals are. It is about retiring early, debt-free living, or buying your dream home. Turning them into specific objectives that lead to tangible changes help to do this. You should visualize what you actually want and give your financial destination direction and focus.

The milestones on the journey are measurable goals. They help you measure your level of achievement and identify when you arrive at the point of financial destination. Having specific milestones and targets will enable you to see how far you have come, celebrate your victories along the way, and adjust if needed. The metric is the equivalent of a compass ensuring that you keep on track.

Goals you can achieve act as pegs for your dreams so that they are firmly rooted into the world of realities. It encourages you to evaluate yourself in terms of the resources, skills, and surroundings that push your dreams towards attainability. Just as anchoring a vessel to prevent its drift in turbulent waters, setting achievable goals helps you fix your financial vessel at one point.

The relevant goals act as an anchor for your financial journey that guides you through a wider path in life. Your vision for finances should be in line with your ideals, way of life, and future goals. It is significant to ensure that your goals are relevant to what drives your purpose in order to keep you both motivated and fulfilled.

Ticking clocks will create a time bound goal to push you into action. These goals give you a feeling that there is a time constraint hence setting deadlines for achieving your financial success. Setting timelines defines what's important, helps avoid distractions during the trip and builds you up with responsibility.

Why do SMART goals matter, then? Aspirations are organized under them and become specific goals. They are like a compass, guiding you as you go and eventually directing you towards your financial goal. Setting SMART goals helps motivate you to focus on realistic expectations that meet what you financially want and what you live for; and also encourage constant actions in pursuit of your aspirations. These act as motivators encouraging you to have fun with the milestones in your journey and keep you from burnout.

How To Create SMART Financial Goals

Specificity - Define Your Targets

Start by being highly specific about what you want to achieve. Avoid vague goals like "save more money" or "get rich." Instead, ask yourself: What do I need to save for, and how much do I need? For example, "Save $20,000 for a down payment on a home within the next two years." The key is to have a clear, well-defined financial target.

Measurability - Quantify Your Progress

Make your goals measurable by assigning numbers and metrics to them.

This enables you to track your progress and know when you've achieved your objectives. For instance, instead of saying "reduce debt," specify "pay off $5,000 in credit card debt by the end of next year." This allows you to measure your success and stay on course.

Achievability - Ensure Realistic Goals

Ensure your financial goals are achievable. Set the bar high, but also be practical.

Don't aim for something that's beyond your means or timeline.

For instance, if you're earning $60,000 a year, it's not realistic to set a goal of saving $1 million in a year. Instead, opt for goals like "Increase annual savings from 5% to 15% of income over the next five years." It's ambitious yet attainable.

Relevance - Align with Your Values

Make sure your financial objectives align with your broader life goals and values.

A meaningful financial goal should be relevant to your aspirations.

For example, if you value family, you might set a goal to "Save $15,000 for a family vacation in three years." This links your financial target to a deeper sense of purpose.

Time-Bound - Set a Deadline

Every SMART financial goal should have a clear timeframe.

Without a deadline, it's easy to procrastinate. For instance, instead of saying "invest in stocks," specify "Invest $10,000 in a diversified stock portfolio within the next 12 months." This time-bound aspect creates a sense of urgency.

Write It Down

Now that you've gone through each element of SMART, write down your financial goals.

It's essential to document them, whether in a journal, on your computer, or a vision board. The act of writing makes your objectives tangible and serves as a constant reminder.

Review and Adjust

Regularly review your financial goals. Life circumstances change, and so should your goals. Periodic assessment ensures that your objectives remain relevant and in line with your evolving needs and aspirations.

Mastering the Art of Self-Discipline

Mastering the art of self-discipline is paramount to wielding a mighty sword of personal power, a skill that empowers individuals to conquer obstacles, transcend limitations, and shape their destinies.

It's a captivating journey of self-mastery, where one harnesses the inner strength to stay committed to their goals, even in the face of distractions and

temptations. Self-discipline, in its essence, is not mere willpower but a profound understanding of one's own desires, decisions, and the unwavering determination to follow through.
Self-discipline is a multifaceted concept that reaches deep into the core of human psychology.

The ability to master yourself is the big sword you must carry with you in order to face and overcome challenges. One can achieve greatness by shaping one's destiny.

The journey is like no other; it's the adventure of conquering oneself through self-mastery. In this quest for self-discovery and transformation, an individual embraces the power within them which allows them to stand the test of time as they persevere despite the many dist. In its entirety, self-discipline consists of one's understanding of oneself, desire, decision and unyielding will power to follow it through.

Self-discipline is a complex term which permeates through the heart into the depth of the human soul. Basically, it is the ability to abstain and remain focused on far-reaching dreams.

This is not about giving in to what feels good but instead choosing paths that advance you towards bigger goals.

An individual can only be able to achieve self-discipline when they are able to identify the cravings they want to avoid as well as the distraction they want to free themselves of. This is a kind of a self-knowing pathway whose objectives are to know what you value most, establish realistic objectives, and take decisions consistent with the objectives set forth.

It involves deferred gratification, which is, postponing immediate benefits in favor of future returns.

Moreover, being self-disciplined entails developing a reliable and efficient strategy or routine. However, this is more than mere reliance on will power, rather, the design of a conducive environment and structure for achieving such goals. That can mean establishing a well-defined work space, dividing a complex project into small tasks and building an everyday schedule that facilitates work efficiency.

Self-discipline is also an art of not giving up when one faces some obstacles. Individuals experience problems and failure at some point in life; however, discipline helps an individual to rise above all these, learn from the mistake made and focus on one's goal without having any doubts. That's basically keeping a growth mentality when you view obstacles as chances of improvement.

Self-discipline is deeply connected to motivation and purpose. When you have a strong "why" behind your goals, it becomes easier to stay disciplined.

Your desires are fueled by a sense of purpose that propels you forward, even when the path gets tougher.

The Power of Self-Discipline

Self discipline is an outstanding and transformative attribute which can open up our hidden talents, help us realize what we want in life, and bring true satisfaction and happiness in our lives. This is a feature that goes beyond time and culture and touches every person whether rich or poor in every era of life. Self-control goes beyond being a virtue; it drives us to do tremendous things which lead us through hurdles, climb high points, and determine ourselves for a desired ending.

Basically, self discipline is the power to govern one's behavior, feelings and cravings for an objective that will benefit later on.

The deliberate choice to give priority to what is really important even when you have an urge for instant satisfaction or diversion. Self-discipline stands out as the compass leading us towards the way of sustained success and personal accomplishment in a world where we are continuously encouraged to indulge ourselves with short term pleasures.

Self-discipline has a significant effect on individual and professional development which makes it one fascinating concept. As much as self-discipline can be a great obstacle, it helps us to set targets without considering any impediments. However, we remain focused on maintaining these efforts, for over time, it makes a difference. Be it in a career pursuit where one needs to rise to the top position, being good at some skill or simply the pursuit of health, we need self-determination to drive us to reach for better.

In the realm of personal development, self-discipline acts as a powerful tool for overcoming self-limiting beliefs and transcending comfort zones. It enables us to confront our fears, take calculated risks, and embrace change with resilience and determination. The process of self-discipline often involves pushing our boundaries, be it in terms of learning, physical fitness, or emotional intelligence.

This continuous self-improvement cycle propels us to explore our full potential, uncovering talents and abilities we might have never realized we possessed. One of the unique features of self-discipline is its ability to foster consistency.

By adhering to a structured routine and maintaining self-control, we avoid the pitfalls of erratic behavior and distractions. This consistent effort, over time, results in a compounding effect, where small, daily actions lead to significant, long-term results. This is often referred to as the "aggregation of marginal gains," a concept popularized by Sir Dave Brailsford, the former performance director of British Cycling.

In his approach, the emphasis was on making tiny improvements in various aspects of the sport, leading to substantial overall performance enhancements. Self-discipline facilitates this concept in our personal lives, allowing us to build a virtuous cycle of success.

The power of self-discipline extends beyond personal achievement and delves into the realm of resilience. It equips us with the mental fortitude needed to weather life's storms. When facing adversity, those with strong self-discipline possess the capacity to stay focused, maintain a positive attitude, and persevere through challenging times. This resilience is often the differentiating factor between success and failure, as it enables individuals to adapt to changing circumstances and emerge stronger on the other side.

Self-discipline can also be appealing because it helps individuals to think creatively and innovatively. It goes against the notion that discipline hinders innovation as it gives direction and inspiration for us to realize our creativity powers. Through self-discipline, we are able to control our impulses and distractions, and help us develop the necessary mental area to indulge in deep learning and creative problem-solving. There have been some great innovations and works of art that have resulted from mixing discipline with creativity at this specific intersection.

Throughout the historical tapestry of mankind, many bright personalities have shown that strength is in discipline. Such people who were insatiably curious and had perseverance exemplified how self-discipline could change the course of a person's life. People have used their self-control to make lasting impacts on society as well as motivate other societies for centuries now.

Self-discipline is highly important in today's world where one faces continuous distractors. Our daily routines are filled with such distractions as unending temptation from social networks, daydreaming, or the illusion that we need to complete dozens of tasks within one period of time.

Nonetheless, people who discover self-control as an essential capability are able to move through a digital age on their own terms. They are able to withstand the temptation of immediate fulfillment and see clearly what they really need.

Chapter 3

Emotional Intelligence and Wealth

Emotional Intelligence (EI) is a concept that has gained significant recognition and prominence since the early 1990s. It represents a multifaceted capacity that goes beyond traditional intelligence (IQ) and encompasses the ability to recognize, understand, manage, and effectively utilize emotions in various aspects of life. This essay provides an in-depth exploration of the history, components, and applications of EI, as well as its impact on personal, professional, and educational realms.

The roots of emotional intelligence can be traced back to early psychological theories.

Visionaries like Charles Darwin and William James emphasized the significance of emotions in human adaptation and survival. However, the explicit term "emotional intelligence" was coined by Peter Salovey and John Mayer in the early 1990s.

It gained widespread recognition through the work of Daniel Goleman, whose book "Emotional Intelligence" brought the concept to the mainstream. Since then, research and understanding of EI have continued to evolve.

The Role of Emotional Intelligence in Decision Making

Emotional Intelligence (EI) is increasingly recognized as a vital component in the decision-making process. It influences how individuals perceive, evaluate, and respond to various situations, shaping the quality of their choices. This essay delves into the multifaceted role of emotional intelligence in decision making, exploring its impact from self-awareness to interpersonal interactions and its relevance in both personal and professional contexts.

Self-awareness, a fundamental aspect of EI, is the cornerstone of effective decision making. It involves the ability to recognize and understand one's own emotions and their implications. In decision making, self-awareness enables individuals to evaluate their emotional state and its potential influence on the choices they make. For instance, someone with high self-awareness can identify when they are feeling stressed, anxious, or overly excited, and they can factor this awareness into their decisions. This introspective knowledge helps in steering clear of impulsive, emotionally-driven choices.

Emotions often fluctuate and may lead to impulsive decisions if not managed effectively. Self-regulation, another component of EI, plays a critical role in decision making by enabling individuals to control their emotions and maintain composure, especially in high-stress situations. It involves strategies like deep breathing, time management, or positive self-talk to mitigate emotional reactions.

When emotions are regulated, individuals can think more clearly and objectively, leading to more rational and well-informed decisions.

Empathy, the ability to understand and consider the emotions of others, is pivotal in decision making involving multiple stakeholders.

In personal and professional contexts, considering the perspectives and feelings of others can lead to more informed and fair decisions. For instance, a manager with high empathy may be better equipped to make choices that consider the well-being and motivations of their team members. This can lead to improved collaboration and overall decision quality.

Effective decision making often involves collaboration and communication.
The social skills component of EI aids in navigating social situations with finesse, building rapport, and resolving conflicts. These skills contribute to successful decision outcomes by facilitating productive discussions and negotiations.

In a professional context, a leader with strong social skills can gather input from team members, align their interests, and reach decisions that are more widely accepted.

Conflict is an inherent part of decision making, and emotional intelligence can be a valuable asset in resolving disputes. Understanding the emotions underlying a conflict, both in oneself and others, allows for more constructive approaches to resolution. Emotionally intelligent individuals can de-escalate tense situations and find mutually beneficial solutions, thus preventing decision-making processes from becoming gridlocked.

In both personal and professional life, emotional intelligence is instrumental in building and maintaining strong relationships. Trust is a critical element of collaborative decision making. People with high EI are often better at building trust, which can lead to smoother and more successful decision outcomes. Trust enables open communication, reduces skepticism, and fosters an environment where decisions are viewed more positively.

Emotional intelligence also aids in recognizing and managing cognitive biases that can distort decision making.

Common biases, such as confirmation bias (seeking information that confirms preconceptions) or anchoring (relying too heavily on the first piece of information encountered), can lead to poor decisions.

Emotionally intelligent individuals are more attuned to these biases and can make conscious efforts to mitigate their influence, leading to more objective and rational choices.

Factors Influencing Consumer Spending Patterns

Emotional Spending

Spending on feelings is a deep-seated part of human habit. It involves psychology, studying our thoughts, buying things we want or need, and understanding how each person handles their problems in different ways. Emotional spending means buying things and acquiring possessions because you are feeling upset or for whatever reason. It's like shopping when sad as a way out of it. This phenomenon manifests in various forms and degrees, playing a pivotal role in shaping individuals' spending habits.

The source of spending money based on feelings can be traced through the complex area where human emotions come from. When people feel worried, scared, or emotionally upset, they look for ways to find comfort. For some people, going shopping is a way to relax and feel better for a little while. It helps them forget about their problems in life during that moment.

In our minds, getting something new can make us happy. It sets off a part of the brain that releases dopamine; this makes you feel good for a short time and brings pride in what has been gained. This brain response builds a loop that links shopping with emotional help. People feel happy when they shop because it makes them less stressed and more relaxed, so they keep doing it to get those good feelings back again.

The idea behind "retail therapy" is that shopping helps heal emotional problems. This way of dealing not only happens when you buy something; the whole experience, from looking in shops to paying for it, helps create a happy feeling. When we spend money on things to feel better, the items bought are like real reminders that get us lost in self-comfort. This gives a wrong feeling of control and peace when going through hard times, instead of producing a false balance.

Emotional spending isn't just a personal reaction to feelings inside us. It is also heavily affected by outside influences, like rules and ideas in society that we must follow. In cultures that see expensive things as a sign of success or joy, people might have the urge to spend money on their feelings.

Moreover, the idea of shopping being a fun thing to do or a way for people to express themselves helps strengthen how it ensures our emotional happiness. Such activity might lead us, maybe when we are enjoying some retail therapy that brings joy and relaxation from our daily stresses, which other times gives a platform towards making purchase decisions based not only on practical needs but also driven by one's urge as a rising sense of self-importance.

Today's consumer culture, fueled by ads and news stories, makes us feel stronger about how we use our money. Ads often show products as ways to solve emotional problems, telling us we can be happier or better in social situations if we buy certain things. Being around these messages all the time can make spending to feel emotions normal. It doesn't seem strange or just a one-time event anymore, but socially accepted behavior instead.

While spending money to feel better might provide short-felt ease, its lasting effects can be detrimental. Money worries, more things being bought, and depending on buying stuff from stores may happen. People who spend money on emotions might get stuck in a loop. They keep looking for approval by buying things they don't need, and while it may feel good temporarily, it results in ongoing unhappiness because that redemption is short-lived.

Understanding and dealing with emotional spending is a mix of being aware, managing emotions well, and knowing about money. Use better ways to handle stress, like reflecting on your feelings or engaging in physical activity. This helps last longer than spending money on things when you're feeling emotional. Better choices help keep our future good! Additionally, enhancing financial literacy helps individuals grasp the repercussions of impulsive purchases and promotes responsible budgeting.

Peer Pressure

Pressure from friends has always been, it not only changes our decisions but also deeply affects how we use money. We all want people to like and accept us, so we often buy things that may not be needed but help us blend in or stand out. Knowing how group pressure affects our buying decisions is about exploring the world of social activities, understanding the thin line between being like others and doing what's unique to each person. It's also about grasping how our minds work when making choices.

Our choices about what to buy are often connected with the people we hang out with. We often watch the likes and actions of other people, trying to find hints on what's liked or thought okay by society. This thing happens a lot during our teen years when we really want friends to like us. This sets up habits that last all of our lives about buying stuff.

Finding the right balance between fitting in and keeping our own identity is very important when it comes to dealing with pressures from friends or classmates. We might want to spend money like our friends even if it goes against what we like or good money sense. This happens because people care about fitting in with their group. Worrying about standing out or being seen as different becomes a big reason to spend money on things that help with social life instead of helping in practical ways.

The effect of peer pressure on what people buy can be really strong. The worry of being left out or the appeal for acceptance by others starts mental actions that shape our choices. The hope of getting good responses from others becomes a strong motivator. It often outweighs thinking about what we need or how to manage money wisely. In this complicated dance, the feeling of being accepted socially can be more important than thinking about how to spend money wisely.

People often buy things because their friends want them too. This goes beyond just usefulness; it's also a way to show we belong and our standing in society. Things like fancy stuff or cool gadgets turn into a way to show off our connection with a certain group of people or way of life. We buy these things because they help show who we are on social media.

We keep wanting more attention so we spend more money.

When we spend money because of our friends, it can give us a short feeling of friendship. But it can also have long-term effects on how we handle money. Trying to copy the spending habits of others can give us money problems and maybe debt. Wanting to please others through what we buy can use up important things we need. This can stop us from being financially good for a long time.

Handling the maze of peer pressure in buying choices needs a careful mix of fitting in with friends and being free. Being strong against things from outside means learning to know ourselves better and trust in what we believe is important. Talking about money goals and spending responsibly with our friends can help our social groups move towards wise buying. We support each other in making good choices, instead of just doing what others want us to do.

Effective Advertising and Marketing

Advertising and marketing have this remarkable ability to make us want things we didn't even know we needed. It's like a magic spell that turns desires into reality, convincing us that we can't live without that latest gadget or that luxurious experience. Let's take a stroll through the captivating world of advertising, understanding how it works its enchantment on our minds.

Have you ever noticed how certain ads grab your attention, making you stop in your tracks? That's the first trick – capturing your focus. Whether it's a flashy image, a catchy slogan, or a heartwarming story, advertisers know how to make us look their way.

Once they have our attention, the real magic begins. Advertisers are like storytellers, weaving narratives around their products or experiences. They don't just sell a phone; they sell the promise of staying connected effortlessly. It's not just a pair of shoes; it's a ticket to feeling stylish and confident. They plant seeds of desire in our minds, making us imagine a better life with their offerings.

Have you ever wondered why some ads make you laugh, while others tug at your heartstrings? That's because advertisers are experts at playing with our emotions. They know that if they can make us feel something – whether it's joy, nostalgia, or even a touch of FOMO (fear of missing out) – we're more likely to connect with the product on a personal level.

Here's where the real magic trick happens. Advertisers have a way of making us believe we need something urgently, even if we didn't think about it a moment ago. Imagine a sleek advertisement showcasing the latest smartphone features – suddenly, your current phone feels outdated, and you find yourself craving an upgrade. It's not about fulfilling a necessity; it's about creating a perceived need.

As we soak in these messages, our behavior starts to shift. The desire planted by the ad transforms into action. Maybe you find yourself browsing online for that product, or perhaps you take a detour to that new coffee shop because its commercial made the brew look irresistible. Advertisers guide our steps, turning their crafted desires into real-world actions.

Consider the world of fast fashion – those trendy, affordable clothing brands that seem to have a new collection every other week. Their ads, filled with stylish models and vibrant scenes, create an illusion of a constantly evolving wardrobe at your fingertips. The desire? To stay on top of the latest trends without breaking the bank. The reality? Your closet might be bursting, but the craving for the next 'must-have' item persists.

Advertising doesn't just stop at the individual level; it ripples through society. Trends sparked by clever marketing campaigns can become cultural phenomena. Think about how a catchy jingle or a memorable slogan can become part of our collective memory, shaping the way we perceive and desire certain products or experiences.

Awareness is the key to navigating the influence of advertising. Understanding that the desire stirred by an ad may not align with genuine needs empowers us to make conscious choices. It's about distinguishing between what we truly need and what has been artfully presented as a need.

Lack of Financial Literacy

The lack of financial knowledge often starts with gaps in education and societal structures. Many people reach adulthood without a strong understanding of budgeting, investing, or interest rates. Limited financial education perpetuates a cycle where vital skills for navigating finances stay underdeveloped.

Moreover, the reluctance to talk openly about personal finance adds to a culture of silence. In environments where money matters aren't discussed, individuals may grow up without exposure to practical aspects of managing finances, leading to a significant gap in understanding.

The consequences of financial illiteracy extend into various aspects of economic life. Without a clear grasp of their financial situation, individuals struggle with budgeting, often resulting in overspending, debt, and overall financial instability.

Financial illiteracy also hampers decision-making on investments and long-term planning. Lack of knowledge about savings, retirement, and investments can prevent individuals from growing their wealth and securing their financial future.

Beyond the tangible impact on finances, the burden of financial illiteracy takes a toll on mental and emotional well-being. The stress from financial uncertainty affects mental health, creating persistent anxiety about bills, unexpected expenses, and an uncertain future.

Addressing financial illiteracy requires a comprehensive approach, focusing on education and awareness. Integrating financial education into school curricula equips individuals with the skills to navigate personal finance. Community programs, workshops, and online resources also play a crucial role in raising financial literacy levels.

Encouraging open discussions about money helps break the stigma surrounding financial matters. Creating spaces for individuals to share experiences and seek advice fosters a supportive environment, empowering people to take control of their financial destinies.

Recognizing the impact of financial illiteracy is the first step toward financial empowerment. Acknowledging root causes, understanding consequences, and actively seeking solutions pave the way for a more financially literate society. Financial education becomes a catalyst for broader economic stability and resilience.

The Fear of Missing Out - FOMO

The fear of missing out, or FOMO, originates from our intrinsic need for social connection and belonging. As social beings, we crave involvement in the collective narrative, dreading exclusion from shared experiences. This anxiety intensifies in the era of social media, where glimpses into others' lives amplify the sense of missing out on exciting events and opportunities.

Social media platforms act as windows into others' worlds, fostering FOMO. As we scroll through meticulously crafted posts, we witness the highlights of peers' lives, creating an urgency to keep up. The fear of not measuring up to seemingly extraordinary lives becomes a driving force, compelling impulsive spending on things we may not genuinely need.

FOMO often leads to impulsive spending, where the fear of missing out overrides thoughtful consideration. The urgency to be part of the moment drives spur-of-the-moment purchases, from the latest gadget to trendy outfits or event tickets. This behavior, fueled by FOMO, can have lasting consequences on financial well-being.

The emotional toll of FOMO is significant, influencing mental well-being. Constant exposure to others' seemingly exciting lives breeds dissatisfaction, contributing to a cycle of comparison and discontent. The drive to alleviate this discomfort through spending creates a feedback loop, reinforcing the connection between emotional relief and acquiring possessions or experiences.

To navigate FOMO, cultivating mindfulness and resisting impulsive spending is crucial. Setting clear financial goals and priorities creates a roadmap for spending decisions. Creating a budget aligned with values helps allocate resources intentionally, reducing the impact of FOMO on financial health.

Developing contentment with our own journey is key. Recognizing that social media often portrays curated moments rather than the full spectrum of reality helps temper the allure of comparison. Cultivating gratitude for what we have fosters a mindset shift away from fear-based spending.

Building resilience against FOMO involves understanding that every opportunity or experience is not one-size-fits-all. Embracing the uniqueness of our own path and finding joy in authentic connections serves as a powerful antidote to FOMO-driven spending. Shifting focus from external events to internal fulfillment allows us to redefine notions of success and happiness.

Lack of Budgeting

Imagine your finances as a puzzle, and each piece represents a part of your hard-earned money. Now, what if some pieces are missing or don't quite fit together? That's a bit like what happens when people don't have a budget – a clear plan for how they're going to use their money. Let's explore why not having a budget can lead to spending money on things they don't really need.

A budget is like a roadmap for your money. It helps you decide where your money should go, making sure you cover the important stuff first. Without this roadmap, it's like setting off on a journey without a destination. You might end up wandering and spending on things that catch your eye, but not necessarily on what you really need.

When you have a budget, you can clearly see how much money you need for essentials – things like rent or mortgage, groceries, and bills. These are the puzzle pieces that should fit snugly together because they are crucial for your daily life. But without a budget, it's easy to lose track of how much money should go into these essential pieces, leaving gaps that can cause financial stress.

Let's imagine Susan, who doesn't have a budget. She gets her paycheck, and without a plan, she starts spending on things here and there – a coffee on the way to work, a new gadget because it caught her eye, and a meal out with friends. Before she knows it, a big chunk of her money is gone.

Now, let's think about what Susan forgot. She didn't set aside enough for her rent, which is a crucial piece of the puzzle. When rent day arrives, she realizes she doesn't have enough money. That's a tough spot to be in! Susan now has to find a way to cover her rent, maybe by borrowing money or skipping other important things.

Not having a budget can lead to spending on things that seem fun or tempting at the moment but don't align with what's truly important. It's like trying to complete a puzzle with missing pieces – there are gaps in your financial picture, and you might end up stressed and struggling to make ends meet.

This lack of planning often leads to unnecessary expenses on items that provide short-term pleasure but don't contribute to long-term financial stability. Without a budget, it's easy to forget about saving for the future or dealing with unexpected expenses, leaving individuals vulnerable to financial surprises.

Having a budget acts like a shield, protecting your money from being scattered in different directions. It helps you focus on what matters most and ensures you have enough for the essentials. With a budget, you're less likely to end up in a tricky situation where you're forced to cut back on vital expenses because you spent too much on non-essentials.

Discretionary Spending

Personal finance theory involves discretionary spending, which refers to that part of your salary that is free from paying off debts or bills for items like food, shelter, and utilities. It stands for the availability of extra money that can be used to buy non-essential goods and services at one's will and pleasure. With regards to this element of expenditure, it includes all sorts of discretionary spending like eating out, recreation activities, hobby costs, clothes purchase and traveling.

Spending on discretionary matters makes them happy that their day has not been boring. It is an avenue through which they go to cafes, take a vacation, pursue leisure, buy some non-essential things like clothes or electronics.

Discretionary spending enriches and spices up our lives but it must be properly managed. Spending in excess in this category results in an unbudgeted budget, the accrual of loan, failed saving plans, and lack of financial stability. Thus, people need to find a way to enjoy some free time without jeopardizing their long-term financial stability.

Managing discretionary spending properly implies providing a smaller portion of earnings for non-indispensable expenditure, keeping track of spending, and being conscious of what is really profitable, valuable and joyous in terms of consumption.

Therefore, individuals can separate wants and needs and set their financial goals so that all discretionary spending is in line with the overall financial objectives of individuals, which will help them have a secure life for themselves and make it prosperous. The world that's full of speed and consumption doesn't take time to think about what to spend or when to stop. They include, however, unnecessary indulgence which are the small pleasure one may opt to add in their life, which if not taken seriously, could cause a lot of damages financially.

Dining Out

One of the most common forms of discretionary spending is dining out. Whether it's the allure of a cozy restaurant on a Friday night, the convenience of ordering takeout during a hectic workweek, or simply the temptation of that aromatic coffee from the corner café, these indulgences can add up.

Dining out not only drains your wallet but also detracts from the joys of home-cooked meals, where you have control over ingredients and portion sizes. Excessive dining out can leave your budget with an unsavory taste.

Entertainment

Our desire for entertainment is entirely understandable; after all, who doesn't appreciate a good movie, an electrifying concert, or the thrill of video games? Yet, these sources of amusement often come at a cost. Spending on movies and concerts, subscribing to multiple streaming services, or acquiring the latest video games can turn a leisure activity into a financial burden. In a world teeming with digital content, it's crucial to discern between meaningful entertainment and frivolous spending.

Hobbies And Recreation

Hobbies and recreation are avenues for personal growth and relaxation, but they can quickly become a sinkhole for finances if unchecked. Gym memberships, sporting activities, and various hobbies can lead to ongoing expenses.

While investing in one's well-being and interests is commendable, excessive spending in this category can undermine your financial stability if not adequately managed.

Clothing And Accessories

Fashion is a dynamic and expressive aspect of our lives. However, the pursuit of the latest trends, designer labels, or accumulating an abundance of clothing and accessories beyond our basic needs can leave our closets cluttered and our finances strained. When fashion choices become excessive, it's essential to consider the true value and necessity of these purchases.

Travel

Leisure trips, vacations, and weekend getaways offer an escape from the routines of daily life, allowing us to explore new places, cultures, and experiences. However, the allure of travel can lead to impulsive spending, from extravagant vacations in exotic locations to frequent weekend getaways. These travel expenses can contribute to a significant drain on savings and hinder financial progress.

The Impact of Unnecessary Spending on Financial Well-being

Budget Imbalance

Excessive discretionary spending can throw your budget into disarray. It's like navigating a ship without a steady course – when a significant portion of your income is allocated to non-essentials, there's less room for meeting essential financial obligations. These essentials include rent or mortgage payments, utility bills, groceries, and loan repayments. As a result, you may find yourself juggling to make ends meet, a situation that can lead to stress and financial instability.

Imagine, for a moment, your income as a limited resource, akin to water in a vessel. When you pour too much of it into the discretionary spending bucket, there's less left for the essentials, and you might eventually find the vessel empty or running dangerously low.

Debt Accumulation

The seductive allure of discretionary spending can often lead to the perilous path of debt accumulation.

Credit cards, with their seemingly limitless purchasing power, can become a double-edged sword. Impulsive spending on items you don't truly need can quickly accumulate, leaving you with mounting credit card debt. These debts, often accompanied by high-interest rates, compound over time, turning seemingly harmless purchases into financial burdens that are difficult to shake off.

Debt, when left unchecked, becomes a heavy anchor, weighing down your financial vessel, making it harder to navigate the sea of life's uncertainties.

Missed Savings Goals

Consider the opportunities missed due to unnecessary spending. The money spent on non-essential items and activities could have been allocated toward achieving important savings goals.

Whether it's planning for retirement, saving for a down payment on a house, or investing in education, these goals often require a disciplined and strategic approach to accumulate the necessary funds. Unnecessary spending diverts financial resources away from these goals, making them more elusive and prolonging the time required to achieve them.

Reduced Financial Security

One of the most profound impacts of excessive discretionary spending is reduced financial security. A lack of savings or a diminished emergency fund leaves you vulnerable when unexpected expenses or emergencies arise. It's akin to setting sail without life vests – when a financial storm hits, you may find yourself ill-equipped to weather the turbulence. Whether it's a medical emergency, a sudden job loss, or a home repair, the lack of financial security can turn a manageable setback into a crisis.

Reducing Discretionary Spending

Creating a detailed budget is the cornerstone of discretionary spending. A well-structured budget assigns a specific allocation for discretionary expenses, setting clear boundaries on how much can be spent on non-essential items and activities. By tracking expenses within this allocation, individuals gain insights into their spending patterns, identifying areas where adjustments can be made to ensure financial well-being.

Distinguishing between wants and needs is a pivotal step in reducing discretionary spending. It requires an honest evaluation of what truly constitutes an essential purchase.

Prioritizing needs means focusing on necessities like rent or investment, groceries, and utility bills before allocating funds to non-essential items. This shift in mindset can prevent impulsive spending on items that, in the grand scheme of financial health, provide limited value.

In today's digital age, subscriptions to streaming platforms, gyms, and various services have become commonplace. Reviewing and canceling unused or redundant subscriptions can free up financial resources. It's about paying only for what you actively use and ensuring that your subscriptions align with your current lifestyle and interests.

A simple yet effective way to reduce discretionary spending is by embracing meal planning and cooking at home. This practice not only helps in controlling food expenses but also encourages healthier eating habits. By reducing dining out expenses, individuals can savor the satisfaction of a well-cooked meal without breaking the bank.

When it comes to shopping for clothing and other purchases, adopting a smart approach can yield significant savings. This entails keeping an eye out for sales, utilizing coupons, and comparing prices. Being a discerning shopper ensures that you get the most value for your money, while also preventing impulsive buying.

Entertainment doesn't have to be synonymous with extravagant spending. Exploring low-cost or free alternatives can provide just as much enjoyment. Parks, museums, community events, and DIY hobbies offer affordable and enriching experiences. By discovering such alternatives, individuals can reduce their discretionary spending while still enjoying life to the fullest.

The Role of Passion and Purpose in Money Management

The topic of money management touches us on a personal level and has far-reaching implications to our day-to-day existence.

Financial decision making is not only about balancing books and budgets, but about shaping the future of individuals and enterprises alike. More often than not, however, such important components of our lives as purpose and passion are overlooked.

Let's start with passion. In this case, passion makes the choice or behavior of a person driven most of the time. This also applies in money management. For example, if one is passionate about an aim such as achieving early retirement, start-up, travel around the globe, one may consider that passion as very effective in financial habits.

It will force you to save more money, not overspend and invest wisely so that your dream could come true. Another way to go is that you take your passion and explore different facets of finance. This might mean getting into stocks, real estates among other things and this is as a result of you catching a "fire" because of your desire to realize a particular financial objective.

But passion alone isn't enough. That is why purpose does. This is because purpose allows financial decisions to be directed and given a sense of purpose. It's about knowing what makes you want to have control over your finances, and how it fits with your overall aspirations in life. Is there a way you keep money to ensure a stable life for your family? What about helping you fund the charity projects that you care so much about and living without debts?

The "why" of your financial decisions is made clear through the motive.

When making a financial plan, purpose has meaning other than accumulating wealth so you attain what is important to you. This is what propels one to take such decisions with regard to their values and dreams. For instance, your objective could be to invest in greener and environmentally friendly deals as far as a situation arises whereby you are interested in saving the environment. This aligns your passion and purpose, creating a meaningful path to financial success.

Balancing passion and purpose in money management is crucial. It's not just about accumulating wealth; it's about ensuring that your financial decisions resonate with your inner motivations and the larger picture of your life. Passion fuels your drive, while purpose provides the roadmap. Passion and purpose can also influence your risk tolerance.

If you're passionate about a high-risk, high-reward investment, your purpose might be to build wealth quickly. On the other hand, if you're passionate about stability and security, your purpose may revolve around ensuring a comfortable retirement.

Your relationship with money is deeply personal, and it's influenced by your values, dreams, and what truly matters to you. It's not just about dollars and cents; it's about shaping the life you want to lead.

Understanding Your Emotional Relationship With Money

People are emotionally attached to money, most of which originate from their childhood issues, peer pressure, and own perception. Money can be a source of comfort and strength to some people, but for others, it may lead to feelings of stress, guilt, or lack of sufficiency. Impulsiveness, a characteristic rooted in our brain's complex interplay of emotions and cognitive processes, can significantly impact various facets of life, including financial well-being.

It refers to the tendency to act on immediate desires without adequate forethought or consideration of consequences. This innate human trait, influenced by both genetic and environmental factors, plays a pivotal role in decision-making and can exert a profound effect on personal, professional, and financial outcomes.

The brain's prefrontal cortex, responsible for executive functions such as impulse control, continues to develop into early adulthood. This area interacts with the limbic system, which governs emotions. The delicate balance between these regions shapes our ability to make decisions.
Impulsivity often arises when the emotional brain overrides the rational prefrontal cortex, leading to hasty actions driven by immediate rewards or the avoidance of discomfort.

Impulsiveness can manifest in various aspects of life, affecting relationships, career trajectories, and overall well-being. In personal relationships, impulsive decisions may strain connections as actions driven by momentary emotions can have lasting consequences. Professionally, impulsivity may lead to abrupt career changes or decisions that undermine long-term success.

The connection between impulsiveness and financial well-being is particularly pronounced. Impulsive spending, a common manifestation, can result in accumulating debt and hinder the ability to save for future goals. Individuals with higher levels of impulsivity are more likely to engage in risky financial behaviors, such as making impulsive investments or neglecting long-term financial planning.

Impulsive individuals may struggle with delayed gratification, opting for immediate rewards even when a patient approach could yield more significant benefits. This behavior, if unchecked, can hinder the accumulation of wealth and financial security. Understanding the neural underpinnings of impulsivity is essential in addressing its impact on financial decision-making.

By recognizing the interplay between emotional responses and cognitive control, individuals can implement strategies to mitigate impulsive tendencies, fostering more deliberate and financially sound choices.

The first step while managing and controlling one's financial life is to understand these emotional ties.

Intense feelings such as financial burdens, debts, or uncertainty of the future can easily be triggered. Emotional intelligence aids people in appreciating and managing such feelings appropriately.

People can address financial pressure using their courage by budgeting on some expenditure or seeking help from experts.

Impulsive buying due to emotional gratification can be checked by emotional intelligence. People typically end up in such situations mainly because of their emotions, for instance due to a need to relieve stress in themselves or just self-rewarding. This is where emotionally intelligent individuals come in handy because they are able to recognize such triggers and take a moment to think before making deliberate purchases that are aligned to their long term financial plans.

Balance between living at the moment and ensuring personal financial security in future. It could mean that some people would go with instant gratifications at the expense of long-term financial purposes for instance or even the opposite whereby these individuals would save intensely and sacrifice their momentary enjoyments.

Such emotionally intelligent persons may evaluate their values and take reasonable financial goals.

Conflicts often arise between partners over money because it plays an important role in every relationship.

It is important to navigate these financial discussions with emotional intelligence. It communicates a message of what financial objectives, priorities, and shared duties will be discussed with partners or family members. Intelligent emotions allow in creating areas of understanding and compromise supportive of economic health for partnerships.

Unexpected expenses, losing employment, and failing investments can be emotionally challenging. Emotional intelligence allows people to cope with such failures by admitting their own emotions, asking for help, and putting together plans on recovery.

Emotional intelligence allows people to cope with such failures by admitting their own emotions, asking for help, and putting together plans on recovery. Emotionally intelligent people overcome such failures by recognizing emotions, acquiring help, and creating strategies for recuperation.

There are two crucial factors of emotional intelligence; resilience and adaptability which allow people to recover from financial challenges.

Our relationship with money is mostly influenced by societal and cultural aspects. Irrational financial decisions may be caused by consumerism, social comparison, and peer pressure. It gives resistance to others' pressure and facilitates making decisions that are based on one's inner drive. It allows one to assess how society and culture affects one's financial conduct.

Emotional intelligence is important in financial decision making. The heuristics also provides people with information about these emotional biases which cause poor decisions such as loss aversion (losses weigh more than gains) or overconfidence.

Therefore, recognizing and controlling these prejudices will help people with their logical and well-founded financial calculations.

Managing Stress and Emotional Spending

A crucial parameter related with finance decisions is linking stress and emotional spending. Therefore, emotional intelligence is central towards deciphering, handling as well as reducing the impacts of stress-related uncontrolled spending by people who are often driven by emotions.

This paper examines the complex linkage of stress, emotional spending and use of EQ for better financial options.

Life has stressful elements and their influence on financial decisions is huge. Impulsive spending may be used by people under stress as a way of dealing with emotions.

Emotional spending is the provision of a temporary solution to feelings such as stress; however, this usually ends up causing monetary pressure in the long run. However, identifying the linkage between stress and emotional spending is an important step towards promoting better financial status.

Emotional intelligence includes understanding feelings to solve problems, managing emotions, or controlling them in a healthy way to achieve certain personal goals or solve life problems. Such sensitivity includes comprehending the psychological effect of tension. Individuals with high EQ, however, pay closer attention to their emotional responses, which enable them to respond rationally, rather than reactively, to stress. When this happens, they should be able to identify stress as a major emotion that causes sudden expenditures and intervene before commencing on any unsound financial commitments.

Managing stress is closely associated with the self-regulation aspect of emotional intelligence. High-stress situations may induce negative emotions in people with high emotional intelligence. Such people have strategies such as deep breathing, mindfulness, and time management which they use against negativity. This enables one to cope and reduces their urge to indulge in emotional spending.

146

Mindfulness under stress is promoted by emotional intelligence among many other things. An emotionally intelligent person can stop and think of how the emotions will affect their bank accounts before giving in to them. The impact of the financial aspects as a result of making the choice is weighed.

Such a mindfulness may discourage frivolous expenditures and encourage thriftiness.
Such people also make more correct links between financial decisions and their futures. They should be able to monitor stress and curb emotional spending to keep their economic choices in line with their principles and goals. This involves making provision for tomorrow, minimizing debts, as well as cutting on excess expenses incurred as a result of stress related feelings.

Emotional spending induced by stress produces more stress that is financial in nature thus compounding on the already existing financial strain. Instead of this, emotionally intelligent people realize that there are stress triggers and they come up with better ways to deal with emotions. Adopting this proactive approach may help enhance financial well being.

However, financially stressed emotionally intelligent people are likely to use emotional support and professional guidance. They know that they should approach financial advisers, therapists, and other support networks for advice on addressing the roots of stress. Such collaborative approaches give rise to more lasting financial remedies and stress reducing measures.

Cultivating Emotional Resilience for Financial Success

Financial success is often viewed through the lens of numbers, investments, and savings. However, a lesser-explored yet equally essential component of financial well-being is emotional resilience. The ability to withstand the emotional challenges that financial matters bring, and to adapt and thrive in the face of adversity, is fundamental to achieving financial success.

In this essay, I delve into the multifaceted aspects of cultivating emotional resilience for financial success, exploring how it impacts our financial journeys, decisions, and overall well-being.

Emotional resilience is the capacity to bounce back from adversity, adapt to challenging circumstances, and endure emotional strain without becoming overwhelmed. In the context of financial success, it means maintaining a sense of emotional well-being despite financial setbacks, market fluctuations, or monetary pressures.

Financial stress is an inescapable aspect of life. Be it a sudden job loss, unexpected medical expenses, or volatile market conditions, financial stress can significantly impact individuals and their families. Cultivating emotional resilience involves recognizing and managing the emotional responses to financial stress. For instance, a family facing unexpected medical bills might experience anxiety and worry.

Emotional resilience enables them to acknowledge these emotions, seek support, and develop a plan to address the situation with resilience.

Financial setbacks can be disheartening, affecting both financial goals and emotional well-being. A small business owner, for example, might face a downturn in the market, leading to reduced income. Cultivating emotional resilience in this situation means acknowledging the disappointment, adjusting expectations, and seeking alternative income streams or strategies without succumbing to despair.

The financial markets are known for their volatility. An investor, watching the value of their portfolio fluctuate, might experience fear and anxiety. Emotional resilience allows investors to weather market volatility without making rash decisions driven by fear. It encourages a long-term perspective, recognizing that market fluctuations are part of the investment journey.

It is necessary to develop emotional resilience, including adhering to a strict discipline regarding matters of finance. As an example, a husband and wife with a goal of buying a house may find it difficult not to spend money on temporary pleasure. Resilience emotionally enables them to remain true to their financial goals, control urges and avoid decisions that move away from the long term plan.

One of them, in their search for emotional resilience, turns either to their friends or even financial advisors. A financial advisor could, for example, help a newly graduated person in debt, who is still emotionally unstable to handle student loans properly. Insights and guidance on how to deal with the financial situation without going into a depression is available in support networks and professional counsel.

Well-being and emotional resilience go hand in hand. People who value personal care, mental health, and emotional stability can more easily survive through any financial crisis.
To cope with the emotional fatigue, a single parent dealing with numerous responsibilities can take part in activities such as exercising, meditating, and even consulting a therapist.

It is necessary that financial success be continuous learning and adapting. Embracing new ways of life through emotional resilience. For instance, an individual looking for a career change has to be emotionally strong and hardy to help him or her cope with changes during the transition process. As a result, it makes them stick to their route of success as it pertains to finances in this case. Setting reasonable goals or reasonable expectation ties also underlies emotional hardiness.

In addition, it means to purchase a home when a young couple begins to have a family. However, such an achievement could be realized in years. They are able to have patience because they comprehend that it takes both time and money to achieve success.

The Secret Strategy to Overcome Impulsiveness

Mindfulness Practices

Mindfulness involves being fully present in the moment without judgment. Meditation and deep-breathing exercises are tools that promote self-awareness, allowing individuals to observe thoughts and emotions without immediate reaction. By regularly practicing mindfulness, one can develop a heightened awareness of impulsive tendencies.

The deliberate focus on breath or specific sensations creates a mental space between stimulus and response, enabling individuals to choose deliberate actions over impulsive reactions. This increased self-awareness empowers individuals to manage their responses more effectively and make conscious decisions aligned with their goals.

Pause Before Acting

The act of pausing before taking action serves as a crucial intervention in impulsive behavior. It provides a moment for individuals to engage their prefrontal cortex, the brain region responsible for rational decision-making. This brief pause allows the emotional brain, which often drives impulsivity, to settle.

During this time, individuals can evaluate potential consequences, weigh alternatives, and consider whether the action aligns with their long-term objectives. The intentional delay introduces a valuable element of reflection, helping to break the automatic cycle of impulsive reactions and fostering more thoughtful, strategic responses.

Set Clear Goals

Establishing clear, well-defined goals provides a roadmap for behavior. When individuals have a clear vision of their long-term objectives, it becomes easier to resist impulsive actions that may jeopardize progress. Breaking these goals into smaller, achievable steps creates a sense of direction and purpose.

Each decision can then be evaluated in the context of these goals, guiding behavior toward actions that align with overarching objectives. This goal-oriented approach not only fosters discipline but also reinforces the idea that impulsive choices can hinder progress toward meaningful achievements.

Create Structured Plans

Developing structured plans for daily tasks or projects serves as a preventive measure against impulsiveness. Plans provide a clear outline of necessary steps, reducing the likelihood of spontaneous, impulsive actions. When individuals follow a predetermined plan, they are more likely to stay focused on the task at hand, minimizing distractions that could lead to impulsive decisions. The structured nature of plans also encourages a systematic approach, fostering a sense of control and organization that counters impulsive behaviors.

Seek Feedback

Consulting with others before making decisions introduces valuable perspectives that may not be immediately apparent. Seeking feedback creates a collaborative decision-making process, reducing the risk of impulsive actions driven solely by individual biases or emotions.

External input provides a broader view of potential consequences and alternative solutions, serving as a valuable counterbalance to impulsive tendencies. The act of considering multiple viewpoints fosters a more thoughtful decision-making approach, reinforcing the importance of careful consideration over impulsive reactions.

Establish Routines

Daily routines contribute to stability and predictability in one's life. When individuals follow consistent patterns, it creates a structured environment that minimizes the chaos that can trigger impulsive behavior. Routines instill a sense of order and familiarity, reducing the likelihood of impulsive decisions driven by the need for immediate gratification or escape from uncertainty.

The predictability of routines provides a stabilizing influence, allowing individuals to navigate challenges with a greater degree of composure and strategic thinking.

Delay Gratification

The ability to delay immediate rewards in favor of long-term benefits is a cornerstone in overcoming impulsiveness. Delaying gratification requires individuals to envision and prioritize future goals over instant desires. This practice strengthens the cognitive processes associated with self-control and patience.

By consciously choosing delayed rewards, individuals reinforce the idea that impulsive actions might compromise more significant future gains. This cultivated discipline contributes to a mindset that values strategic thinking and thoughtful decision-making over impulsive, short-term satisfaction.

Reflect on Values

Regularly reflecting on personal values serves as a powerful deterrent against impulsive actions that may conflict with one's core principles. Understanding and reaffirming one's values provides a moral compass, guiding decision-making in alignment with deeply held beliefs.

When faced with the potential for impulsiveness, individuals who reflect on their values are more likely to choose actions that are consistent with their ethical framework. This reflective process adds a layer of conscientious decision-making, making it more challenging for impulsive behaviors to override foundational values.

Healthy Lifestyle Choices

Maintaining a healthy lifestyle contributes significantly to cognitive well-being, positively impacting decision-making and emotional regulation. Regular exercise, proper sleep, and a balanced diet support optimal brain function.

Physical well-being is closely linked to mental and emotional states, and disruptions in these areas can contribute to impulsivity. Engaging in healthy lifestyle choices not only enhances overall resilience to stress but also provides a foundation for more stable, thoughtful decision-making. When the body is well-nourished and rested, individuals are better equipped to resist impulsive actions driven by fatigue or heightened emotional states.

Accountability Partner

Having an accountability partner creates a supportive network that encourages responsible decision-making. Sharing goals and progress with someone trusted establishes a system of checks and balances.

Knowing that there is someone aware of one's objectives adds a layer of responsibility, making it less tempting to succumb to impulsive actions.
The accountability partner can offer insights, feedback, and encouragement, serving as a valuable resource in moments where impulsiveness might be a risk. This external support system reinforces the commitment to strategic thinking and helps maintain a focus on long-term goals.

Chapter 4

The Modern Budgeting Approach

Accordingly, modern budgeting should not be a rigid and only-one-size approach. The system is flexible as it accounts for individual differences in their financial situations. Its incorporation of multiple income streams, evaluation of both recurring and variable charges, and ultimately achieving surplus is all geared towards wealth creation. Individuals who conscientiously record their incomes and expenditures are able to understand their patterns well enough to make sound choices.

A modern type of budgeting has become attractive due to their power to turn a time value into actual money. It gives power to the people to use the money they have efficiently, protecting them from the hassles of taxation as well as unnecessary expenditure. However, those who are able to implement this technique do not simply sell labor time in exchange, they smartly trade a portion of the money for their time which makes it possible to concentrate on hobbies, interests and one's life mission.

The significance of assembling and developing a contingency fund which is such a buffer against sudden financial blows, cannot be overemphasized under this methodology. This approach encourages individuals to save and invest on a continual basis with the ultimate aim of achieving financial sustainability in the future. Reviewing and re-adjusting a budget on a regular basis allows an individual to tailor spending to changing monetary conditions.

More accurately, modern budgeting is an ever-changing financial device that promotes self-discipline within parameters.

This way, people are able to make right decisions, decrease financial pressure while making real steps

for reaching their dreams. It's a practical and powerful guide showing you how to be richer with each dollar which you manage not to spend.

Utilizing Digital Budgeting Apps for Financial Success

Using digital money tools and apps is a good plan for anyone who wants to have more control over their finances without having too many hard words. These useful tools, found on your phone or computer make the difficult job of looking after your money easier. Instead of using many big words, they choose to keep things simple. This makes taking care of money easy for anyone.

A smart friend to help you on your money adventure, without getting mixed up. These apps are like digital money guides, breaking down the hurdles that may scare you. They aren't just tools; they are your personal money helper. They make it easy for you to handle budgeting in the world of finances.

These digital tools for budgeting are wonderful because they're easy to use. You don't need a degree in finance to understand them. They use words you understand, small ones that have a big effect. Picture a computer helper that shows you your spending, money coming in and saving goals easily without using hard words. It's money handling without any troubles.

If you use these tools, it's like having a money friend with you all the time. This online friend doesn't only watch how you spend money; it helps guide smart choices about your cash. It's like having a money helper always ready, 24/7.

Let's explore how to actually use digital tools for budgeting. These tools often have easy-to-use features that let you sort your costs without any trouble. Instead of fighting with spreadsheets and hard-to-understand formulas, you can just put your buys as "groceries," "utilities" or "fun". It's like putting money in neat little boxes. This makes it easy to see when and where we spent our cash.

These apps often give helpful reports and pictures. No need to go through lots of numbers; instead, you get colorful charts and graphs that show your money situation clearly. It's easy-to-understand money information that lets you see trends and patterns in how much you spend.

Digital budgeting tools are also really good at setting and watching money goals. If you're saving for a holiday, new toy or money box in case of an emergency, these apps can help keep your goals safe. They change your targets into smaller parts, giving a plan to reach financial success. It's like using a money GPS, showing you how to get where you need with simple instructions.

These tools usually come with reminders and alerts too. Don't worry about forgetting to pay bills on time or spending more money than you planned. Your money helper on the computer will remind you softly to keep going. It's like having a reliable friend who helps to make sure you stay good with money.

A big plus of online budgeting tools is that they're easy to use. They follow you around wherever you are, whether it's on your phone, tablet or computer. No more reasons to forget updating your budget; it's directly in your hands. This easy access lets you decide how to use your money quickly. This promotes understanding of finances in real time.

You Need a Budget - YNAB

Many people often don't have enough money and freedom because they lack a planned way to manage their finances. "You Need A Budget" (YNAB) changes how people handle their money. It uses a plan called Zero-Based Budgeting (ZBB). It changes how people use and make choices about their pay.

Zero-Based Budgeting is a basic but powerful idea. It works on the idea that each earned dollar needs a set goal, so no money is left sitting around or untraced. It changes budgeting from just tracking costs to a complete plan that matches each dollar with specific money aims and priorities.

The trip to the world of ZBB starts when money comes in. Picture your paycheck as a group of hardworking people, ready to help with money matters. The first thing to do is assign a job for each dollar. In the world of YNAB, this is about setting up money for different areas like home costs, food shopping, utility bills and more. We also save it to pay back our debts. Each dollar works to reach a shared goal together.

The main point of ZBB is to reach a completely equal outcome. This isn't about spending all your money; instead, it is making smart moves with resources to balance income and costs completely. It's like handling your team of dollars so that no dollar is wasted - each one helps you to be financially successful.

On the YNAB platform, you find out that ZBB is not a hard or unbending system. Life is always changing and so are your money situations. You might face surprising costs or your money coming in may change. YNAB tells people to change and move their dollars in the way they need them. If you get more money, this will be given jobs too. These jobs can include putting away savings, investing or buying something special for yourself.

What makes ZBB different is its idea of giving power to people and spending money mindfully. By giving each dollar a clear task, you become more aware of your money priorities. It changes budgeting from a tight task into a free way to reach your targets. With YNAB, you not only check spending but also change your money future.

In the busy world of today's money management, having up-to-date information is very important. "You need a budget." (YNAB) helps with this by adding its real-time linking feature. Users can easily match their bank accounts for automatic import of transactions without any problems. This makes sure your budget is always current, showing the latest money dealings.

Real-time matching gets rid of having to put in things by hand, lessening the chance of mistakes or bad math. When you do business, it easily fits into your money plan. This shows what's happening with your finances right now and is always up to date. This feature not only saves time but makes your budget more accurate. It lets you make smart choices with the most recent money facts. In the fast-changing world of personal money matters, a recent and correct budget is very important for good control over how much we spend.

Setting and following money plans is important for good finance planning, YNAB knows this by adding a strong goal tracker tool. If you want to save for emergencies, get rid of debt or plan a dream trip, YNAB helps people set goals and go after them in money matters.

This tool gives a plan for your money travels, letting you lay out clear goals and watch how far you've come over time. By giving your money a clear objective, you make each purchase meaningful. This helps to match up what you spend with the broader goals of your finances. Setting goals changes how you make a budget. It turns it from just managing money expenses into something important for making your dreams come true, giving us meaning and direction with our money matters.

In a time of always moving and 24/7 connection, ynab suits modern life with its mobile apps for both android and ios devices. The ability to handle your money when outside is very helpful. It makes sure that what you think about and decide with regards to

169

how much money you have does not only happen on a computer in your home but can also be done anywhere.

On the YNAB mobile apps, you can open your budgets and make changes without any trouble. You also review financial details from smartphones or tablets at any time. This ease lets people easily manage their money without being in one place. It helps them plan better and care about saving or spending cash anytime, anywhere. Using your phone, when you're shopping or going to work or organizing money during a holiday trip helps keep track of everything related to finances.

Knowing how you spend money and make it grow is key in making good choices about your finances. The ynab's reports and insights feature gives budget analysis a fresh start. It lets people see how they are doing with their money better by giving them full details in the form of charts or pictures about what is happening to it financially.

These reports show how you spend your money, listing where it's going. They also point out possible places to change spending habits for the better.

Charts show trends and patterns, making it simple to understand how you handle money. Just a quick look is all that's needed! With this data, users can make smart choices. They know what to change and how they have to adjust spending on money matters like budget planning. Reports and information change money management from a quiet job into an active way of learning about finance.

They give users the power to make their choices with cash better by showing them how they spend, save or invest.

Debt can be a big problem in money matters, but YNAB solves this with its debt repayment feature. This tool gives users the chance to systematically sort and pay off their debts, helping them find a way towards freedom from money problems.

YNAB makes people deal with their debts directly by arranging and putting first the ways to pay them back. By using money wisely, people can quickly get rid of their debt. This tool not only helps people take back charge of their money situation but also makes them feel good as they see clear growth towards being debt-free. In YNAB, paying off debt changes a big job of dealing with money owed into an organized path to be free from it.

Knowing about money is important for good choices with cash, and ynab understands the need to give us wisdom. The site does more than just help with money management. It includes many learning tools to educate users and make them better at handling their finances.

These resources include articles, guides and interactive things that talk about all sorts of money matters. They start from the basics like making a budget to more advanced methods for getting richer. YNAB helps people know about money skills so they can handle their own finances with confidence.

This feature turns YNAB from just a money management tool into a complete learning place about finances. It makes sure users not only deal well with their money but also grasp the key ideas that lead to financial success.

On how to use YNAB for iOS, go to the App Store on your iPhone or iPad. For Android, go to the Google Play Store on your Android phone or tablet.

Look for "You Need A Budget" and get the app. Make sure you get the real version to be safe and have all of its features.

When you start the app, it will ask you to make an account. Give the needed details like your email and a safe password. YNAB cares about privacy, so your information is safe.

YNAB usually gives a free trial period. Pick the plan that fits your needs, be it a free trial or one you pay for. Subscription plans might have extra features, but the main functions are often in the free trial.

To get the best from quick matching, link your bank accounts to YNAB. This lets the app bring in transactions on its own, so your budget always stays current. YNAB uses strong security like banks to make sure your money and bank details are safe.

After linking your accounts, now it's time to arrange for a budget. YNAB uses a method called zero-based budgeting. That means every dollar you have should be given something to spend it on.

Make groups for your spending like house costs, food shopping, power bills and saving money.

Divide your money into the groups you made. This step is very important to make sure your money plan matches what you want financially. YNAB asks you to be thoughtful with your money, giving each dollar a task.

As you make purchases or receive income, log transactions in the app. For linked accounts, transactions may be imported automatically. Regularly review your spending against your budget to stay on track.

Take advantage of YNAB's goal-tracking feature. Set specific targets for saving or debt reduction, and monitor your progress over time. This adds a layer of motivation and direction to your financial journey.

Dive into the Reports and Insights section of the app. Gain a comprehensive understanding of your spending habits through detailed charts and reports. Use this information to make informed decisions about your financial priorities.

Download and log in to the YNAB mobile app on your smartphone or tablet. This allows you to manage your budget on the go, ensuring that you stay connected to your finances no matter where you are.

Explore the educational resources within the app. YNAB provides articles, guides, and interactive content to enhance your financial literacy. This knowledge empowers you to make informed decisions about your money.

Budgeting is not a static process. Regularly review your budget, track your progress, and adjust as needed. Life changes, and so should your budget to adapt to new circumstances or goals.

By following these steps, you'll be well-equipped to access and use the YNAB app effectively. Remember that consistency is key, and actively engaging with the app will yield the best results in gaining control of your finances.

Goodbudget

Goodbudget is a budgeting software based on the envelope method. Picture your money like a bunch of digital envelopes marked with separate spending areas such as food, fun or payments. This easy comparison helps you to see where your money is spent and how much is remaining in each area.

In Goodbudget, making digital envelopes is like giving tasks to your money. You choose how much you put in each envelope, depending on what is important to spend. This picture helps you spend money smartly and stops spending too much in certain spots.

It's easy to put your money info in Goodbudget. The app helps you to put this money into different sections, making sure you know how much is for buying things. It's like splitting your paycheck into separate online jars for different reasons.

Goodbudget makes it easy to keep an eye on what you're spending. You can type in your own spending or connect to your bank accounts for automatic transaction import. This part makes sure that your online letters correctly show what you spend. This helps to keep track of money, so it's easier not to go over budget.

Goodbudget knows that people need to change things. It connects with many devices, so you can handle your budget easily using a phone or tablet. You also can use it on computers anywhere anytime! This means you can look at your money plan and change it anywhere, so the information about spending cash is always close by.

The app doesn't just stop at tracking your money - it helps you understand how much and where you spend. Goodbudget makes reports and information easy for users to understand. Pictures and short reports help you understand how much money you're spending. This gives power to make smart choices about your finances. It's like having a clear guide for your money trip.

Goodbudget offers options to cater to different preferences. The free version includes essential features for budgeting enthusiasts. If you're looking for extra perks like unlimited envelopes, syncing across devices, and email support, there's a Plus version available. This flexibility allows users to choose the plan that best suits their budgeting needs.

Pocket Guard

PocketGuard's transaction tracking feature forms the backbone of the app's functionality. By connecting safely to your bank accounts and credit cards, PocketGuard brings in all money transactions automatically. This gets rid of the need for you to write things down by hand, making sure your money records are correct and current. This real-time tracking shows your spending habits well. It gives helpful information about how you handle money.

After transactions are brought in, PocketGuard sorts them into different spending groups. This grouping isn't just done by itself, you can also change it. It lets the app get a better understanding of how much money you spend. The in-depth look helps you find where most of your money goes. This allows careful choices about changing how much to spend and saving for the future.

Making a budget in PocketGuard is something you can do on your own and change as needed. People can set limits on how much they will spend in various areas. This shows what is most important to them financially. Then, the app watches your real spending compared to limits you set beforehand. Alerts warn you when your spending reaches or goes over budget limits, helping to focus on money awareness and powering up staying in control.

PocketGuard's bill tracking feature makes the often ignored job of handling regular payments easier. The app helps you know upcoming payments by finding and watching bills. This forward-thinking method lets you arrange your spending plan to cover these set costs. This reduces the chance of missing payments and connected fees that come with them. Putting all your bills together makes for a more neat and less worrisome money life.

PocketGuard motivates people by helping them set and see their saving goals. People can set certain goals, like making a safety money reserve or saving for a trip. The app shows your money goals in a picture format. This helps you keep going and focused on reaching those financial dreams of yours.

PocketGuard looks at how much money you bring in after cost checking. Knowing when and where you get your money helps you see how well off financially you are. This tool helps to improve the flow of money. This makes sure you have enough funds for your commitments and goals related to savings.

For people managing debts like loans or credit cards, PocketGuard's tool for tracking how to pay back money owed is very useful. It shows you a simple view of how your debt lessens as time goes on. This being open about money not only encourages good behavior with finance, but also shows as a picture race that you made for taking care of your finances.

In PocketGuard versions with credit score tracking, you get information about how good your credit is. Using the app to check your credit score often, lets you see what effects it has on how healthy that is. So you can act quickly and make those parts better. PocketGuard connects better with other financial tools, making it the full budget assistant we need. It covers daily money spending and bigger overall health of finances too.

To use Pocket Guard, start by downloading the PocketGuard app from the app store. Once installed, you'll need to link your bank accounts and credit cards to allow the app to fetch your financial transactions.

After linking your accounts, PocketGuard will display your recent transactions. Review and categorize any uncategorized transactions to ensure accurate budgeting.

Set up your budget by specifying spending limits for different categories. You can customize these limits based on your financial goals and priorities.

Regularly check the app to monitor your spending against your budget. Adjust your spending habits as needed to stay within your budgetary constraints.

Define savings goals within the app, whether short-term or long-term. PocketGuard will help you visualize your progress, motivating you to contribute regularly toward your financial objectives.

Ensure that all your recurring bills are accurately identified by the app. Use the bill tracking feature to plan for upcoming payments and avoid late fees.

If your version of PocketGuard includes credit score monitoring, take advantage of this feature to stay informed about your credit health and identify areas for improvement.

Make it a habit to regularly check the app for insights, updates, and alerts. The more actively you engage with PocketGuard, the better it can assist you in achieving your financial goals.

Debt Snowball

The first part of the debt snowball method is to make a list of all your debts, no matter how much interest they have. First, we focus on the whole amount owed. This helps plan how to pay it off by sorting debts from smallest to largest. This planned arrangement is a big part of why the debt snowball works well.

Beyond just money worries, the debt snowball takes into account how we feel when paying off debts. Begin with your smallest debt so you can have speedy wins. This first success makes your mind feel good. It helps to push you and gives courage for handling bigger debts with more confidence. It's about creating a feeling of success and using it as energy for the trip to come.

It's important to work on paying off the smallest debt, but don't forget about the bigger ones. Paying the smallest amount on big debts helps keep them under control. This stops extra money problems from happening. This method is like keeping a protective position against bigger opponents and carefully attacking the smaller ones that are easier to handle.

Having a little extra money allows you to pay back faster. By guiding extra money to the smallest debt, you give it a push. This makes its removal quicker and easier. This part is like giving a little help to the underdog in a race, pushing it up and nearer to winning.

The debt snowball gets its name from the compound effect it makes. When you pay off the smallest debt, the money that was used for it is then given to the next smallest debt. This process keeps going, like a big snowball rolling down the hill. It gets bigger and faster as it moves along. Each debt that gets paid adds force, making the snowball keep growing until all debts are cleared.

Instead of being just a one-time solution, the debt snowball is an ongoing and repeating process. It's about paying off little debts, adding those payments to the next one and keeping going through all of them. Doing this many times is like swimming round and round in a pool. The more laps you do, the better you get at swimming because it makes your muscles strong.

The debt snowball understands that the path to freedom with money is not just about figures; it includes attitude too. People start with small debts to gain confidence and strength. It's like getting ready for a big race; you start with easy tasks first and then move on to bigger ones. The debt snowball is like a training program for getting better with money. It helps people to pay off their debts while also making sure they're learning how to manage cash and being strong in the field of finances.

"Honeydue"

"Honeydue", an innovative app for couples, makes handling money easy and fun. It changes the sometimes difficult chore of managing finances into a simple shared task. By connecting your bank accounts, the app combines all of your money details in one simple place to see. This makes sure you're clear and open about how much cash matters impact what happens with it.

"Honeydue's" strong promise to keep your private information safe is very important. Tough computer codes protect your messages and make sure that only you can see personal details. Use "Honeydue" to handle personal and shared costs easily. This tool lets you put expenses in logical groups, this way it's hard for confusion about money stuff.

Make a plan for the money you share with others by making budgets, like paying rent and going on dream trips. Follow how much you've advanced and write notes on invoices to make sure nothing gets lost. Even money you spend alone has a neat spot in "Honeydue". It keeps things organized while making space for your own spending habits.

Use emoji to make buying discussions more fun. After spending money wisely, give a big thumbs-up or have some fun talking about unexpected costs. This helps you and your partner to talk openly more easily.

Set big money goals as a group, like saving for your perfect home or creating an unexpected fund. Celebrate when good things happen, building up a feeling of success and togetherness.

Join groups made for couples who have similar money issues. This will help you talk and learn from each other about your problems with spending, saving or making big amounts of cash. Share tips, join talks or read useful guides to make your knowledge of money better.

"Honeydue" helps start talks about money, leading to fewer fights and stronger bonds between the two.

Get together and take on money tasks as a strong team. Understand how you spend money, make smart choices and keep your budget goals in sight.

Say goodbye to the stress of sharing costs with "Honeydue". The app helps with shared money responsibility, making it easier to work well together financially. It can make the trip towards having the same ideas about finances smooth and fun.

Budgeting Software Tools for Businesses

Ready to revolutionize how your business handles finances? Dive into a world of budgeting software tools designed to streamline your financial strategy. This list covers both general budgeting tools and specialized cash flow forecasting tools. General budgeting tools provide the basics you need, while cash flow forecasting tools take it a step further, helping your business tackle crucial obstacles for lasting success.

Imagine having a financial ally that not only manages budgets but also predicts your cash flow's future twists and turns. Cash flow forecasting tools seamlessly integrate with your budgeting and accounting processes but come packed with robust predictive features. These tools aren't just for today; they're essential companions for navigating the financial landscape in the months and years ahead.

Whether you're steering a small startup or managing a larger enterprise, these budgeting software tools empower you to make informed decisions, ensuring your business thrives well into the future. Explore the synergy of general budgeting tools and advanced cash flow forecasting to unlock a new level of financial control and resilience.

These tools aren't only for today; they are important partners when it comes to handling money problems in the future.

No matter if you run a small business or bigger company, these budgeting tools help you. They let you make good decisions so your business does well in the future. Look at how combining basic money planning tools and more complex cash flow predictions can give you more control over your finances and make them stronger.

Xero

Xero, a famous company that makes accounting software for the cloud has greatly changed how global businesses handle money matters. Known for its easy-to-use interface, strong features and smooth connections, Xero is a top pick for small businesses around the world.

Look at what Xero can do to see how it might change your business money. It carefully watches money movements, giving a complete view with detailed reports and tools to sort things out.
Easily make fancy bills, send them through the internet and help people pay online. This makes handling invoices quicker and easier.

Control buying orders, check supplier bills and automate cost claims for best spending management. This makes handling purchase processes easier.

Make payroll easier and handle taxes for workers well with Xero Payroll. This will ensure quick and correct payments are made in time.

Xero gives businesses the ability to see their financial performance in real-time and get useful information. Dashboards that you can change show important numbers right away. This helps make fast choices based on fresh data.

Make detailed money reports, including profit and loss accounts, balance sheets for assets and debts, and cash flow records. The ability to dig deeper helps with detailed studying and creating plans for the future.

Make and watch budgets for various departments or tasks. Xero's tools help guess future money flow and financial results. This helps with big plans in finance before they happen.

Check important company numbers (KPIs) and watch business health with tools like money spending rate and time to get more cash. This helps businesses stay flexible.

Allow different levels of access for team members to work together safely on money tasks, while keeping data safe.

Make simple jobs like regular bills, paying bills and okaying expenses automatic. This saves time and makes the work better or faster.

LINK bank accounts, set up transaction balancing automatically and lower the chance of mistakes by getting rid of handwritten data entry.
Xero can easily connect with well-known business apps. This makes work easier and helps share data between different parts of a business.

Beyond basics, Xero has special skills made for certain business wants. Project accounting keeps track of project expenses, handles budgets well and creates reports for costs. This helps with having good control over money spent on projects.

Take care of how much stock you have, follow the movement of goods and create orders to buy more. This helps control inventory better.
Keep an eye on getting, wearing down and selling fixed things for proper money reporting to follow

tax laws.For world business, Xero lets you manage transactions in many currencies. It updates exchange rates automatically and makes reports in the picked currency.

Xero helps businesses from all over the world. It gives them local features, tools for following tax rules and supports different languages.
Xero makes jobs easier and gives quick money details. This helps businesses save time to think about important choices.

Reports, analytics and forecasting tools give better understanding of money matters. They help businesses make smarter choices with more control and visibility over their finances.
Xero helps to safely share money details with the team and other important people. This makes things clearer, so everyone has good choices about finances.

Automated workflows and secure access controls reduce mistakes and fraud, which lowers operation costs while lowering money risks.

Xero can change with growing business needs and gives extra features or connections. This makes it big enough for more work, while still being flexible.

Xero's charm goes beyond its powerful features. With an easy-to-use interface that can be used via any web browser or mobile app, it helps people who know different levels of accounting. Its strong safety setup and tight data privacy rules make sure your money info is safe and secret.

Xero provides adaptable payment plans for various business sizes and needs. A free try gives a chance to look at its parts, letting companies check if it's good for them. Lots of training materials, lessons and helpful people make it easier to start using the platform. This helps businesses get best use from this system.

To use Xero, open your internet browser and visit its official website. Look at the various membership deals from xero. Pick the one that works best for your company needs. you might find choices for little companies, growing businesses or existing enterprises.

Press the "start free trial" button for your chosen plan. Xero usually gives a trial time for you to look at its features before buying into a subscription.

Fill out the sign-up form with your business information, such as company name, email and country. Make sure you use a real email address because that's what will be your login name. Make a safe password for your xero account. Check that it has the needed safety features to keep your money information safe.

Look in your email for a message to confirm from xero. Click on the link in your email to confirm you're signed up. Check your xero account after logging in. You'll need to give extra information about your business like the type of industry, how it is set up and the favorite currency.

After giving the needed business details, you can change your xero dashboard to suit it. Add tools or pick a design that you like, so it's easy for you to find essential money information fast. You can link your bank accounts to xero for a better way of checking transactions. This allows your money information to be updated automatically.

Get to know the features and settings of xero. You can look at choices such as billing, cost tracking, money payment and report tools. change settings based on what your business needs. If you have a group working on money jobs, ask them to join in at xero. provide different permission levels to make sure safe teamwork.

Use xero's training resources to your advantage. Xero often gives lessons, guides and online talks to help people use the platform better.

Once your account is ready and arranged, you can begin to use xero for managing money matters. Make bills, watch costs and see the different tools out there to make your business money stuff easier.

Remember, xero's easy to use and wide support help make it available for people with different levels of accounting skills.

QuickBooks

QuickBooks is a very popular accounting software used by small and medium businesses. It helps them manage their money better. The software is easy to use and helps people who know a lot or little about accounting. The dashboard shows important money information in a simple way. It helps you easily move through its different features.

QuickBooks is good because it makes invoicing and getting paid easy. People can easily make professional bills, adding their logo and company colors to give it a personal feel. The program helps make payments online, speeding up the time it takes to pay bills and improving overall money flow control. The ease of making bills with this software makes it very popular.

Keeping track of money spent is made easy with QuickBooks. The software links bank accounts and credit cards. This allows it to get transactions automatically, instead of having to type them in by hand. People can easily group costs. This makes it clear to see where their money is going out. This tool is very helpful for spending money wisely and making plans about finances. It helps businesses use their resources in the best way possible.

QuickBooks makes it easy to do bank reconciliation, which is very important for keeping good financial records. The program helps link bank transactions to account records, making sure everything matches. This not only saves time but also makes less mistakes, helping to make the software trusted for keeping perfect money records right.

QuickBooks makes handling payroll, a complicated and often wrong task, easy. The software correctly works out how much money employees get paid, their taxes and any deductions. People can easily make money slips and pay taxes without any trouble. This also saves time and lowers the chance of compliance problems, making sure businesses follow law rules.

QuickBooks' reporting and data analysis tools help businesses learn important things about their money situation. People can make reports like profit loss summaries, money balance sheets and cash flow statements. These reports are very important in making good decisions and meeting requirements for reporting. They help make the software a complete way to handle money matters.

QuickBooks can connect with other software, making its use more flexible. Businesses can easily link the software with online shopping sites, money transaction systems and customer connection tools. This changeability lets companies adjust QuickBooks to their special needs, making it even more useful in different types of businesses.

Using QuickBooks on the internet is good for businesses that have workers far away or those always traveling. The cloud-based version lets users get their money info from anywhere they can connect to the internet. This feature makes sure that people can work together in real time and share data across many devices. It helps businesses meet their changing needs today.

Security is very important for any accounting program. QuickBooks handles this by using strong protection codes. Important money info is kept safe, and new fixes are given out often to deal with possible weaknesses. People can also add extra security by using more than one method. This makes sure their money details stay safe and are not changed in a bad way.

QuickBooks realizes help might be needed, so it offers full customer support and training materials. You can get help through lessons, online chats and live support if you have any questions or problems with the system. QuickBooks makes customers happy because it's a popular choice for businesses that want good and dependable accounting software. This adds to QuickBooks' charm.

Other budgeting tools for companies are Sage Accounting, Wave, FreshBooks, Casual, Zoho Books, Float, Finmark, OneUp and Futrli.

Look up more about them and pick the one that matches your business needs and money plans. It's very important to know that every solution given by these money management apps and programs has its own restrictions. These tools surely help with managing money for yourself or your business, but it's very important that both regular people and businesses use them carefully. The world of financial technology is always changing, with lots of new things getting better all the time. But, this action also makes problems and mistakes that users should be careful about.

A big problem with apps used for creating budgets is that they may not fit well with the special money needs of people who use them. Some apps don't suit everyone or businesses, and trying to use a single way for all people may make them unhappy. So, a smart move for people is to do deep research before adding any new changes into how they handle their money.

A key part of this study is learning what each app or software program does. Not all features might match what the user wants to do with money, and it's important to find out which ones are most useful. Learn more about them and choose the one that works best for your company. Their money plans should fit with how you manage finances already, so don't forget this in using budgeting apps. To work well, the tool needs to fit smoothly into our daily habits. Some people might find it hard to use some software because of the way they work.

Worries about privacy and safety are also very important in money matters. When people give private money details to these computer programs, it's really important to know how safe they keep that information. People should use apps that follow strong safety rules and coding for protection. This will lower the chance of someone accessing them without permission or leaking data.

It's also important to think about how reliable the customer help is given by the app or software maker. When there are problems with how something works or if things aren't clear, quick and good help can be very helpful in fixing the issues. This makes sure that people have a nice experience using it. People should check reviews and what others say about the customer support of their chosen solution. This will help them understand how quickly it responds and gets things done well.

The always changing technology means that new things and changes are often added. Changes can make things better, but they might also bring unexpected problems. People should be careful before quickly using new updates and, instead, wait for first opinions to show up. This careful method helps people avoid mistakes from using something new too soon. It lets users make smart choices about adding in new features into their money management practices.

Strategic Budgeting to Reclaim Money

Emergency Fund

The cornerstone of financial security is the establishment of an emergency fund. Allocating a portion of your income to build this fund ensures that you're prepared for unexpected expenses, reducing the reliance on credit cards or loans when crises arise. An emergency fund provides a financial safety net, offering peace of mind in times of need.

When creating an emergency fund, it is recommended to take into account the number of months or years it will take you to get another job in case you lose your current job. As a beginner who wants to achieve financial freedom but you are soaked in stress due to financial instability and does not know how and where to start, emergency fund building is the best option to help you save money for emergency cases that may arise. This approach helps you avoid getting into so much debt when there are emergencies and helps you manage your finances accurately for future investments. It is the first thing you must do immediately after receiving your paycheck before even getting into more financially demanding commitments.

Set a target for your emergency fund. This will depend greatly on how much you receive every month and the essential expenses. Irrespective of your situation, you must commit to this because when you lose your job today and you have no money set aside, be it investment or any form of savings, your landlord, your creditor, your bank, or whoever you may owe at that time will not spare you for the reason that you have lost your job.

Set a clear target for yourself. Know how much you receive at the end of the month. Add up all important costs such as housing, meals, travel and payments for utilities. Ask yourself "if I want to have $X in a year, then how much money do I need to put aside every month?". Do the mathematics, and with self-discipline and continuous implementation, you will achieve your target.

Debt Reduction

High-interest debt, such as credit card debt, can be a major financial burden. Allocating extra funds to pay off this debt is a strategic move to save on interest payments and ultimately achieve debt freedom. By diligently chipping away at outstanding balances, individuals regain control over their finances and can redirect those resources toward their financial goals.

Stop borrowing money! Tempted to go for another loan? Hold on. Stop and think. Some people are drawn into debt but still go to borrow money to settle that previous debt. This is just like a vicious cycle. Once you are able to pay the previous one with another debt, the current debt with its interest awaits you.

With this kind of behavior, you will not see yourself improving financially in life. You might even go bankrupt as debts with their high-interest rates will start to pile up. Ask yourself, will going for another loan to settle a previous debt help you get out of debt, or will it sink you further down? You must learn to stop borrowing money, and that means no more loans.

Get your paycheck at the end of the month and calculate your essential expenses. Plan well and assign tasks to any amount of your money. You need to reshape your behavior, your views of money, and your attitude towards debt. If you do, you will see a significant change in your life. Otherwise, if you keep borrowing money, it will just dig you a deeper hole that you might not be able to escape from all your life.

Understand the true cost of borrowing money, like using your credit card. Is it worth it? Think of the long-term. Start bringing cash when shopping. Live on cash. Spend cash, and leave your credit card at home. Stop borrowing and start building for the future.

Keep an eye on where your money goes. Are coffee shops, subscriptions, or bills draining your funds? Tracking your spending is crucial financial advice, a secret to success for many. Successful people understand if their money is working for or against them. Is your money doing what you want? To tackle debt this year, you must know where your money is going. Creating a budget is challenging without a clear picture of your spending. Identify areas to cut back by listing expenses like mortgage, bills, food, transportation, gas, and your children's education. Don't forget to include debt payments in the list.

Consider renegotiating any credit card debt. Try to renegotiate your agreements by proposing a lump sum payment instead of monthly installments, a tactic known as debt settlement. Give them a call and ask for reduced credit card rates, especially if you have a positive payment track record. This could be an opportunity to achieve freedom from debt. Engaging in these conversations may open up possibilities for improved financial terms.

Think about switching utility providers. Certain bills can be lowered, aiding in saving money for debt repayment. These may involve phone bills, cable expenses, electricity, and insurance. Research and compare options. Look for better rates from competitors, and don't hesitate to change to a provider that offers the same quality but at lower costs.

Craft a family budget. Share your debt situation with your family, keeping them informed on your progress. Explain your plan for speedy debt repayment. Be transparent about your real financial state, encouraging their involvement in budget creation and tracking. This is crucial, especially if you're the sole earner. Engage your kids in the conversation, teaching them budgeting and saving strategies early on to enhance their financial skills.

Commit to becoming debt-free. Envision your debt-free life, picturing how you and your loved ones will thrive. Imagine the freedom of living without the weight of debt. This transformative moment begins when you condition your mind and set the intention to achieve financial liberation.

Defining clear savings objectives is pivotal to achieving financial success. Whether it's saving for retirement, a down payment on a house, or education, setting specific goals provides direction and motivation. Automating contributions to these savings goals ensures consistent progress, making financial aspirations more achievable.

Strategic budgeting also extends to investing wisely. Growing wealth over time requires a deliberate approach to investments that align with your financial goals. Whether it's building a diversified investment portfolio or exploring opportunities in real estate or entrepreneurship, informed investment decisions can help you secure your financial future.

How Rich People Make Money With Debt

The problem with most of us is that we think a good job or saving more money is all you need to become rich. This unconscious belief holds many back. Billionaires operate on a different playbook, unknown to many. They were once like you, finding it hard to make ends meet, yet they survived. It's not magic; they planned and implemented what they learned consistently. It's hard work, and you can do it too.

Stop stifling your inner being. You have potential within you that calls for rekindling. Awaken the supernatural being within you and build a thriving future for yourself.

Unfortunately, for many, financial literacy is a recent realization, and now they wish they could go back to their youthful age to start working on their future. This is an emotional yet educative comment. For some old people I've met, this has been their story—lack of financial literacy. I once spoke with a man who shared how he could have built his fortune if he understood finance early. At 48, he started educating himself and implementing the steps he learned. He went from $256,000 in debt with zero savings to fully debt-free with a net worth over $120,000 eight years later. He proudly took that step and is now fast-tracking his investments, owing no one. It's a good feeling.

School systems, designed by governments, aim to make you an employee without teaching financial literacy. A salary is only a subordinate to reduce poverty but doesn't make you financially free. It lies in each of us to start reasoning. It all begins with a change of mindset towards financing. Your future belongs to you, and what you do today will determine it. Stop the excuses and keep working on yourself.

Most people associate debt with negativity, often borrowing money they cannot afford for entertainment, ending up paying much more back. For students, right after getting out of college, they realize the burden of student debt. Once they calculate how many years they have to pay back that debt, they immediately perceive debt as a bad thing, especially when they can't even default on it.

Playing around with debt is not easy; you are taking a huge risk, and a small miscalculation can lead to disastrous consequences.

Many people are now in so much debt that they can't even afford an unexpected $600 bill. However, this distinguishes bad debt from good debt. Debt can ruin your life, make you homeless, and cripple your family if you become reckless. But it can also make you unbelievably rich if you know how it works and how to use it because it is leverage. Leverage is a superpower that can make you rich instantly.

Let's consider this for the sake of example. You buy a phone for $7,000, go to the market, and sell it for $8,000. You made a profit of $1,000. That's not enough, but if you use leverage, you go to the bank, borrow $993,000, and with your additional $8,000, that gives you $1,001,000. You go to your supplier and purchase phones using that amount. You get 143 phones now for $1,001,000.

Now, turn around and sell them to the market for $8,000 each, giving you $1,144,000. But you still owe the bank, right? Go back to the bank again and return their $993,000 that you borrowed and let's say another $25,000 in interest. Now, you are left with $126,000, and after your own deduction of $8,000, leaving you a profit of $118,000. That's how you make money when you don't have money. The bank made their share of the profit, and you also made yours.

This is a major way in which rich people make money. Of course, it's very risky, and you can end up losing everything if not planned well, but you can make more money out of it if you know what you are doing.

You might have heard phrases like 'debt is the root of all evils,' 'never get into debt,' or 'debt is slavery.' To some extent, this is true because when you're drawn into debt, your whole life is affected. While you are trying to pay your debt, your debts are not waiting for you; they are multiplying day by day since no one lends money for free. There is always an interest.

Debt is not as inherently bad as people think. Most of what we have are bad debts. You probably have credit card debt, a car loan, or maybe student debt, and you are thinking if it will take you forever to pay off all these debts. "How on earth is debt something good?"

It might seem a bit confusing because why would someone in debt make money with it? Some people will ask why the rich use debt to make money when debt is supposed to be used by people who do not have more money.

Most people will ask why I need debt to start a business. Of course, this is something that seems impossible. Let's say you want to sell clothes, a very good product with high demand in the market. Normally, you will go to the manufacturing company, buy the clothes, ship them to your country, and distribute them to your clients. But today, that's mostly done online. But here is the big deal. You don't really have to pay for the products to have them first.

In the past years, China has been a great manufacturer of most products, and most companies give you the product with the agreement of paying for it in the future. You might be wondering if this is possible. Yes, it's possible, but you need to build trust with these companies. Once you get the product and sell them, you pay the company back and borrow more products. The best strategy is to tell the company "if you are able to produce more quality products, then I will help you sell them." If they agree, the products will be given to you at a certain price, and if you are able to sell above that price, that will be your profit.

When this strategy works, you are not going to use your own money to buy the products, and this is why selling is a good skill.

Real estate debt is a perfect debt. If you don't have a mortgage, then you are paying extra taxes. Rich people always have multiple mortgages to help them reduce all those deductions. They are able to invest every dollar that is supposed to be used on taxes. Now, let's go the practical way. Let's say you have saved $200,000. That's something big, but ideally, it's just a small amount.

Let's say you find a property that is worth $500,000, which is in bad condition and needs renovation. You head to your bank and get a mortgage by making a down payment of 20% of the cost of the property, which is $100,000. Let's also consider that you are going to spend 10% of the total cost of the property on renovation, and that's $50,000. After your renovation, you head to the bank again for refinancing.

The original cost of the property was $500,000 because it was in bad condition that no one would want to live there, but it has been renovated, and now there are people who want to rent it out, so the market value of that property, let's say now rises to $750,000.

Suppose you get an 80% mortgage, that's $600,000 on $750,000. Out of this money, $400,000 is going to the bank that gave you the mortgage. Now, let's deduct the renovation cost of $50,000 from the remaining $200,000, and this will give $150,000 into your wallet using debt.

That property is now left for you, and you can rent it out to build equity to generate passive income. Can you really say debt is bad after this? Answer that yourself. There is always a bunch of money waiting for you in the bank. Make good use of it.

Chapter 5

Creating a Legacy and Giving Back

Finding Financial Mentors and Role Models

For many beginners, the involvement of mentors and role models has been revolutionary in the financial sphere. Such persons with remarkable personal achievements in other areas become a beacon to navigate through the sea of financial options in some instances.

However, their perspectives are grounded with experience and knowledge; they direct novices from familiar errors to reasonable tactics. The impact is unforgettable, for they do not merely provide knowledge but also bolster one's ability to traverse the challenging arena of financeology. They bring their own stories in most cases characterized by difficulties and these make it possible for learners to identify much more with such teaching.

Mentorship imparts discipline, guides sound investments, and generates tenacity amidst volatility in the marketplace. Instead, individuals are motivated by "rags to riches" tales, revealing that their dreams are attainable. Success stories of these people inspire them to be determined as it is from mere aspiring to action. The part played by the mentors and role models in the financial sphere where a greenhorn is provided with the necessary "tools" for defining his own financial destiny and dream realization can hardly be measured.

It is more than just earning some cash. It is also important to make well-informed and sound financial decisions. This process is greatly influenced by financial mentors and role models who influence it in several ways. They possess experience and expertise. A good number of financial mentors are conversant with financial market matters like investments as well as strategies that may go a long way in assisting you overcome the difficulties. On the contrary, role models are alive and they offer positive examples that make one yearn to emulate them.

Take the example of Warren Buffett, often considered one of the greatest investors of all time. His journey from a young boy with a passion for investing to the chairman and CEO of Berkshire Hathaway is an inspiring story. His wisdom on value investing, long-term thinking, and risk management has guided countless individuals to make sound financial choices.

Mentors and role models can provide personalized guidance. They can assess your unique financial situation, goals, and challenges, tailoring their advice to your specific needs. This personalized approach is particularly valuable in a field where one-size-fits-all solutions often fall short.

A prime example is Suze Orman, a renowned financial advisor. Her expertise in personal finance and her ability to relate to people's financial struggles have empowered individuals to manage debt, save for the future, and invest wisely.

Mentors and role models offer emotional support and motivation. mentors and role models offer emotional support and motivation. Finance can be a daunting and stressful endeavor, especially during market fluctuations and economic uncertainties. Having someone to turn to for encouragement, reassurance, and a fresh perspective can make a significant difference in your financial journey.

Consider the late Maya Angelou, a poet, and author who rose from poverty to international acclaim. Her life story teaches us about resilience and determination, qualities essential in navigating financial challenges.

Where to Find Financial Mentors and Role Models

Finding the right guidance and inspiration is often a crucial step towards achieving your financial goals and securing your financial future. Financial mentors and role models can play a significant role in this journey, offering valuable insights, knowledge, and motivation. This essay explores the various aspects of finding financial mentors and role models, shedding light on their importance and how to effectively seek them out.

Now that we understand the significance of financial mentors and role models, let's delve into where and how to find them.

Professional Networks

In the financial industry, professional networks are a goldmine for mentorship opportunities. Attend industry events, conferences, and seminars to connect with experienced professionals who may be willing to guide you.

Mentorship Programs

Many organizations and associations offer mentorship programs specifically designed to pair seasoned financial experts with individuals seeking guidance. These programs often have structured frameworks for mentorship relationships.

Online Communities

With the rise of the internet, online communities and forums related to finance have become hubs for sharing knowledge and experiences. Engaging in these communities can help you identify potential mentors and role models.

Biographies And Autobiographies

The lives and experiences of successful financiers are often chronicled in biographies and autobiographies. Reading these can provide insights into their strategies and philosophies, making them virtual role models.

Professional Associations

Joining professional associations related to finance, such as CFA Institute or the Financial Planning Association, can connect you with seasoned professionals who are often eager to mentor the next generation.

Educational Institutions

If you're a student or an aspiring finance professional, your educational institution may have resources for mentorship and career guidance. Professors and career counselors can often assist in connecting you with potential mentors.

Social Media And LinkedIn

Platforms like LinkedIn offer opportunities to connect with and follow influential figures in the finance industry. Engaging with their content and reaching out respectfully can lead to valuable mentorship relationships.

Maintaining a Successful Mentorship or Role Model Relationship

Maintaining a successful mentorship or role model relationship is like tending to a garden; it requires care, attention, and a willingness to nurture growth. Whether you're a mentor guiding someone or a mentee seeking guidance, fostering a positive connection is essential for personal and professional development.

Firstly, communication forms the bedrock of any fruitful mentorship. Regular, open conversations allow both parties to share insights, address concerns, and set goals. A mentor should create a supportive environment, encouraging their mentee to express thoughts and ask questions without fear of judgment. Likewise, a mentee should actively seek feedback, providing a chance for constructive dialogue.

Listening is a key aspect of effective communication. A mentor should attentively listen to their mentee's challenges, aspirations, and achievements. By understanding the mentee's perspective, a mentor can offer more relevant advice and tailor guidance to individual needs. Similarly, a mentee gains valuable insights by listening to the experiences and wisdom shared by the mentor.

Trust is another crucial element in maintaining a successful mentorship. Both mentor and mentee need to trust each other for the relationship to flourish. Trust is built over time through consistent actions, reliability, and a shared commitment to growth. A mentor should be dependable and true to their word, while a mentee should be open to receiving guidance and implementing suggested changes.

Setting clear expectations is a foundation for a successful mentorship. Both parties should be aware of their roles and responsibilities. A mentor must define the scope of their guidance, ensuring the mentee understands the level of support they can expect. On the other hand, a mentee should communicate their expectations and goals, fostering a collaborative approach to the relationship.

Flexibility is vital in adapting to the evolving needs of a mentorship. As individuals grow and circumstances change, so too should the dynamics of the mentor-mentee relationship. A successful mentor recognizes the importance of flexibility, adjusting their guidance to meet the evolving challenges and goals of the mentee.

Celebrating successes, no matter how small, is a powerful motivator within a mentorship. Acknowledging achievements reinforces positive behavior and encourages continuous effort. A mentor should express genuine pride in their mentee's accomplishments, while a mentee should recognize the mentor's contributions to their growth journey.

Constructive feedback plays a pivotal role in personal and professional development. A mentor should provide feedback in a constructive and supportive manner, emphasizing areas for improvement while recognizing strengths. On the other hand, a mentee should be receptive to feedback, viewing it as a tool for refinement rather than criticism.

Patience is a virtue that sustains a mentorship through challenges and setbacks. Both mentor and mentee should understand that growth takes time, and setbacks are a natural part of the journey. A mentor's patience in guiding a mentee through difficulties, coupled with the mentee's perseverance in facing challenges, contributes to the enduring success of the relationship.

Maintaining a work-life balance is essential for both mentor and mentee. A mentor should encourage a healthy balance, emphasizing the importance of personal well-being alongside professional pursuits. Similarly, a mentee should recognize the significance of self-care and maintain a holistic approach to personal and career development.

Paying it Forward: Becoming a Financial Mentor

Mentorship is a mutually shared road of experience, knowledge, insight, and wisdom between an individual pursuing guidance and their mentor. This mentorship is important because it can equip the mentee with enough skills and sufficient confidence which allows him/her to make sound decisions.

Mentor-ship provides individual development, education on finance and it turns out to be a turning point for someone's life.

You function as a beacon through the sometimes perplexing and daunting environment of finance. Confidence is an invaluable thing, and you give your mentee this priceless gift. Your role also includes passing on life and financial wisdom. They teach you how to make the right choices when it comes to finances, and show you that dreams do come true. By doing this, you are making a tool that can make you take control of your financial life in your hands.

Mentorship is an individual development pathway. It forces you to revisit your personal spending habits and drives home some vital lessons on personal finance. When you shape someone's future, you make a better version of self. This personal growth has a self-rewarding quality, bringing you closer as a person with your knowledge of money.

However, mentorship entails much more than brain-work. A soul shaking and motivating journey. Becoming a shining light in the life of your partner is always hard but still possible if one is determined.

Watching them blossom into confident individuals, experience the eureka moments as well as seeing the changes in their self-assuredness is rewarding on an emotional level.

Mentorship supports a critical financial literacy that allows people to make sound decisions with regard to earning and securing a solid foundation for their economic life. Giving your information to a mentee empowers them because they will have acquired a skill that goes beyond what you shared during mentorship. It's not about short term monetary issues alone; you're paving the way for their long-term success and financial well-being.

Moreover, mentorship is a transformative force. It has the potential to shape destinies, break generational cycles of financial hardship, and open doors to opportunities previously deemed unattainable. Your mentorship can inspire your mentee to dream bigger, to set audacious financial goals, and to pursue their passions fearlessly.

In becoming a financial mentor, you're not just impacting one life; you're setting off a chain reaction. The knowledge and confidence you impart can ripple through communities, fostering economic stability, and prosperity. Your mentee, influenced by your wisdom and encouragement, may one day become a mentor themselves, continuing the legacy of knowledge sharing and empowerment.

Mentorship is a profound, inspirational, and emotionally rewarding journey. It's about making a lasting difference in the lives of others while experiencing personal growth and fulfillment.

So, if you ever consider becoming a financial mentor, remember that you're not just teaching about money; you're illuminating the path to financial empowerment, one mentee at a time. The impact you create extends far beyond numbers; it touches hearts and transforms lives.

How to Become a Financial Mentor

Becoming a financial mentor is a profound commitment to sharing knowledge, nurturing financial literacy, and making a positive impact. This role offers both personal and societal rewards, but it requires a structured approach:

Assess Your Expertise

Reflect on your financial knowledge and experience. Identify the areas where you excel and where you can genuinely offer valuable insights. It's crucial to have a clear understanding of your strengths and limitations. For instance, if you're well-versed in investment strategies, this could be your forte.

Identify Potential Mentees

Seek individuals who are genuinely eager to learn and who can benefit from your knowledge. Mentees can be family members, friends, colleagues, or even individuals in your professional network. Choose those who are receptive to mentorship and genuinely interested in improving their financial well-being.

Establish Clear Goals

Define the objectives of the mentorship relationship. Have open and honest discussions about expectations, not only with your mentee but with yourself as well. Set clear, achievable goals for both parties. Understand what your mentee hopes to achieve and work together to formulate a plan.

Structured Mentorship

Consider implementing a structured mentorship program with a well-defined timeline, regular meetings, and specific learning outcomes. A structured approach ensures consistency and progress. Having a roadmap helps both you and your mentee stay focused and track progress effectively.

Teaching And Guidance

Share your knowledge and experiences while providing guidance and answering questions. Encourage your mentee to explore and learn actively. This hands-on approach is invaluable in helping them understand the practical aspects of financial management. You're not just a mentor; you're a guide, showing them the way through real-world financial decisions.

Monitor Progress

Regularly assess your mentee's progress and provide constructive feedback. Adapt your mentorship to their evolving needs and goals. By keeping a close eye on their development, you can tailor your guidance to address specific challenges and foster growth effectively.

Challenges and Best Practices

While becoming a financial mentor is rewarding, it is not without its challenges. Effective mentoring requires a nuanced approach and the ability to navigate potential obstacles:

Mentoring is a journey that may not yield immediate results. It requires patience and the understanding that progress can be gradual. It's about guiding your mentee through the learning process at their own pace. Recognize that each mentee is unique. They have their own learning style, pace, and specific challenges. As a mentor, it's essential to adapt your approach to match their individual needs. A one-size-fits-all strategy often falls short in mentorship.

Your actions often speak louder than words. Be a role model in your own financial decision-making. Demonstrating ethical and responsible financial behavior reinforces the importance of integrity in financial dealings.

In financial mentorship, it's not just about the numbers; it's about the ethics and values that underpin financial decision-making. Instill the importance of integrity and ethical behavior in financial dealings. A strong moral compass is as essential as financial knowledge.

Empower your mentee to think critically and make informed decisions. Mentorship is not about creating dependence; it's about fostering independence in financial decision-making. Encourage your mentee to analyze situations, explore options, and make choices with confidence.

Planning for Retirement and Investment

Planning for retirement and investment is a multifaceted endeavor that holds the key to financial security and independence in one's later years. It's a comprehensive strategy that transcends mere savings into a well-thought-out blueprint for a comfortable and fulfilling retirement. Let's explore the various dimensions of this critical financial journey.

At its core, retirement planning involves setting clear and achievable goals. These objectives encompass defining the age at which you intend to retire, determining the lifestyle you aspire to maintain, and estimating the financial resources required to sustain it. Setting these goals is the initial step to frame your financial roadmap.

One of the fundamental elements of retirement planning is creating a budget. This involves a thorough examination of your current financial situation, encompassing income, expenses, and savings. A well-structured budget provides the groundwork for managing your finances efficiently and reallocating resources towards retirement goals.An emergency fund is a cornerstone of financial stability. It serves as a safety net to shield you from unforeseen financial setbacks.

Building an emergency fund equivalent to several months of living expenses is a prudent move, as it ensures you won't need to dip into your retirement savings when unexpected expenses arise. Retirement accounts are instrumental in accumulating wealth for retirement. 401(k) plans, IRAs, and other retirement-specific accounts offer tax benefits and facilitate long-term growth. Contributing regularly to these accounts is crucial to take full advantage of the compounding effect and reduce your tax liability.

Diversification is a key strategy in investment planning. Spreading your investments across various asset classes such as stocks, bonds, real estate, and alternative investments mitigates risk. Diversification is vital because it prevents a single setback from substantially impacting your portfolio. Your risk tolerance should guide your investment decisions. Assessing how much risk you're willing to undertake is a pivotal step.

Generally, younger individuals can afford to take more risks, while those closer to retirement may opt for a more conservative approach to safeguard their accumulated wealth. Consulting a financial advisor can be invaluable in this process. These professionals possess expertise in creating personalized retirement plans tailored to individual financial situations, goals, and risk tolerance. Their insights can provide a significant advantage in crafting a robust retirement strategy.

Periodic reviews and adjustments are essential in retirement planning. As life unfolds, your goals, financial situation, and the market dynamics change. Regularly assessing your plan and making necessary modifications ensures that your strategy remains relevant and aligned with your evolving needs.

Minimizing high-interest debt is another critical aspect of planning. Carrying high-interest debt can impede your retirement savings, as it diverts funds away from wealth accumulation. Prioritizing the reduction of such debt is essential to enhance your financial preparedness for retirement.

Continual education is crucial for staying informed about financial matters, investment options, and market trends. Staying well-versed in these areas empowers you to make informed decisions and adapt to changing financial landscapes.

Planning for retirement and investment is akin to nurturing a tree, a symbol of financial freedom and security. Just as you diligently water a young tree, your consistent efforts in saving and investing lay the foundation for your future wealth. With each financial contribution, you're nourishing your tree of prosperity, ensuring it thrives and grows.

Retirement isn't about ceasing work but having the choice to do so. It's the point when you've tended to your financial garden so well that your wealth starts to grow automatically, outpacing the creeping threat of inflation. Your assets, much like a mature tree, have roots deep enough to sustain themselves, and that's when the real magic happens.

Picture a tree that, after years of nurturing, suddenly doesn't need your constant attention. It's become self-sufficient. This is the moment your investments, carefully tended over time, start to provide for you.

They become your financial shade, offering you comfort, peace, and the freedom to enjoy life without financial worries. This journey to financial security is deeply emotional, for it's about realizing that your sacrifices today are sowing the seeds of a brighter, more secure tomorrow. It's the sense of liberation that comes when your assets stand strong, safeguarding your retirement dreams.

Let this analogy resonate in your heart and soul, driving you to take action. Begin nurturing your financial tree today, water it with savings, tend to it with wise investments, and watch as it grows into a flourishing canopy of security and freedom. Your future self will thank you for your dedication, and the shade of your well-planned retirement will be the most heartwarming reward of all.

Leaving a Lasting Financial Legacy

Financial legacy is an important and deep-rooted issue which goes beyond generations. A wide range of things such as finance, assets allocation, and good intentions are implied in it. The practice is an art of making sure that the riches which people earn in their lifetime live on even when these individuals are no more.

Simply put, a lasting fiscal legacy embodies the enduring principles, faith, and ideologies, which shaped the creator's life or that of an entire family line. Stewarding of one's wealth which entails making informed decisions on how to shape peoples' lives or their heirs, as well as supporting causes close to oneself and the well-being of society at large. The legacy goes beyond just offering financial gifts; it is a form of teaching the benefactor his/her philosophy.

Leaving a financial legacy is a strategic thing which entails careful and proper scheduling of one's income. Wills, trusts, and other documents for smooth transition of properties. They include tax-efficient arrangements aimed at easing the heir's burdens and providing them with an appropriate amount of resources. Utilizing trusts, endowments and philanthropic foundations, wealth can be well managed in a structured and sensible manner.

It's important to recognize that the concept of a financial legacy is not solely for the wealthy. Anyone, regardless of their economic status, can leave behind a legacy through careful planning and

intention. A modest family heirloom, a cherished family recipe, or even a well-documented family history can all be part of a meaningful legacy.

Moreover, a lasting financial legacy extends well beyond the allocation of assets; it encompasses financial education and empowerment. It is about equipping heirs with the knowledge, skills, and mindset to manage and grow their inheritance wisely. This educational aspect ensures that the legacy is not just about wealth transfer but also about imparting the wisdom and acumen to sustain it.

A financial legacy is about perpetuating values. It serves as a living testament to the principles and values that have shaped your life. Your financial legacy communicates what you hold dear, what you stand for, and the lessons you've learned. It tells your descendants and the organizations you support not just how to accumulate wealth, but also how to live a meaningful, principled life. It's an opportunity to mold the character of your heirs, imparting wisdom that extends far beyond financial management.

Leaving a financial legacy is also about supporting future generations. When you pass on your wealth, you provide your children, grandchildren, and future descendants with a foundation for pursuing their dreams and ambitions.

This financial security doesn't merely make their lives more comfortable; it empowers them to aim higher, to take risks, and to explore their potential. Your legacy becomes the wind beneath their wings, propelling them to achieve their aspirations with confidence.

Financial legacy enables you to create a lasting impact that reaches beyond your immediate circle.

Charities associated with education, or other communities of interest would be a good example here. Beyond life, yours does not end in your contributions, instead, society still gains from those contributions. You are a tool of transforming society at the expense of eliminating social problems, building communities and imprinting your footprints onto the global map.

Financial legacy represents a legacy of philanthropy. However, it is not only making money but instead striving to contribute towards betterment of the society. Through developing a financial legacy, you motivate others to emulate such behavior of generosity even after your demise. Philanthropy is contagious and it is important for you to understand this because your own actions set precedence for future generations.

It is also not merely an act of nobility; it is a great act of influence. It's not about your wealth but you have to be sure you leave behind something greater than yourself and wealth for the generations to come as you make them your legacy. It is your value, which lives forever, and shows that one man or woman can change this world for a better life.

The legacy of any financially affluent individual is a unique opportunity with an accompanying responsibility toward shaping the future. Accumulating wealth is actually more than just gathering wealth for individual benefits. Instead, it involves using wealth to raise others up, creating meaning in a person's life as well as inspiring future generations.

Financial legacy matters because it creates a world where the world is more just, generous, and decent. It's a bequest of inspiration, a perpetual reminder of humanity's ability to imprint upon the universe a mark of goodness for eternity.

Bonus

Earn Passive Income Aside Your Monthly Paycheck

In today's economic world, jobs from 9-5 are not the only way to earn. The gig economy has started a new time, giving people many chances to earn passive income. Let's explore how taking on different jobs can lead to more money sources and help you reach financial freedom.

Passive income is money you get from activities that don't need much of your time or involvement after they are set up. Unlike the normal way of trading time for money, passive income sources keep coming in with less work needed after starting. They give a solid cash flow and let you focus on other things too.

There are many jobs at gigs that go beyond direct pay. They offer ways to make extra money without doing more work. Let's explore some common gigs and how they can contribute to your financial well-being:

Freelance Writing:

Freelance writing lets you turn your way with words into income. Write articles, blog posts, or website content for businesses or individuals. Many platforms connect writers with clients looking for quality content, such as Upwork or Fiverr. Write articles, blogs, or content for businesses. Create and sell e-books or repurpose articles for online courses.

Graphic Design:

Graphic design is about making things look good. Design logos, social media graphics, or marketing materials for businesses. You don't need a fancy degree; just creativity and tools like Canva or Adobe Spark.

Design logos, graphics, or marketing materials. Sell customizable design templates or create and sell stock graphics.

Ride-Share Driving:

Become a ride-share driver with companies like Uber or Lyft. Use your car to provide rides to people going from one place to another. It's flexible – you choose when and where you want to drive. Drive for platforms like Uber or Lyft. Referral bonuses for recruiting new drivers or participating in car advertising programs.

Online Tutoring:

If you're good at a subject, offer online tutoring. Help students understand topics they find challenging. Use platforms like Chegg Tutors or Tutor.com to connect with learners seeking your expertise. Provide tutoring services in various subjects. Develop and sell pre-recorded tutorial sessions or educational materials.

Affiliate Marketing:

Promote products and earn a commission on sales through affiliate marketing. Share your unique affiliate link, and when people make purchases using it, you get a cut. It's like being a digital salesperson without handling the products. Promote products and earn a commission on sales. Build niche affiliate websites or use social media to create ongoing income.

Photography:

If you enjoy taking photos, sell them online. Platforms like Shutterstock or Adobe Stock allow you to upload and sell your images. Every download puts money in your pocket – turning your passion into profit. Sell photos on stock photo websites. Continuously earn royalties from the licensing of your images.

Virtual Assistance:

Virtual assistants provide support to businesses from the comfort of their homes. Help with tasks like email management, scheduling, or data entry. It's like being an online right-hand person for busy professionals.

Offer administrative support remotely. Create and sell digital administrative templates or guides.

Real Estate Crowdfunding:

Invest small amounts in real estate projects. Earn a share of rental income or profits without active management.

Social Media Management:

Get Paid to PostIf you're a social media whiz, manage accounts for individuals or businesses. Create and schedule posts, engage with followers, and help build a strong online presence. Tools like Buffer or Hootsuite make it easier.

Web Development:

Build Websites, Build IncomeIf you know how to build websites, offer your services to clients. Help businesses or individuals create their online presence. Platforms like WordPress or Wix make it accessible for beginners.

Online Surveys:

Earn by Sharing Your OpinionParticipate in paid online surveys to earn extra cash. Companies pay for your opinions on products or services. It won't make you rich, but it's an easy way to make a little money in your free time.

Pet Sitting/Dog Walking:

Furry Friends, Fatter WalletLove pets? Offer pet sitting or dog walking services through platforms like Rover. Take care of animals while their owners are away or give dogs a good walk for some extra income.

Fitness Training:

Shape Up Your FinancesIf you're into fitness, offer virtual training sessions. Help others get in shape from the comfort of their homes. Use video platforms to conduct workouts and share your passion for health.

Consulting:

Share Your WisdomBecome a consultant in your field of expertise. Offer advice and insights to businesses or individuals seeking your knowledge. It's like being a paid mentor or guide in your niche.

Event Planning:

Create Memorable MomentsPlan and coordinate events for clients. If you're organized and love details, this gig lets you turn events into unforgettable experiences. Help people celebrate milestones or achieve successful gatherings.

Handyman Services:

Fixing Homes, Filling PocketsOffer home repair or maintenance services. If you're good with tools, help people fix things around their homes. It's like being the go-to person for all things handy.

Language Translation:

Bridge Communication GapsIf you're bilingual, offer translation services. Help translate documents or facilitate conversations between people who speak different languages. It's like building bridges through language.

E-book Writing:

Turn Ideas Into EarningsWrite and sell ebooks on platforms like Amazon Kindle. If you have a story to tell or knowledge to share, publishing ebooks lets you turn your words into royalties.

Interior Design:

Offer virtual interior design services. Help people enhance the look of their living spaces. It's like being an online stylist, guiding others to create aesthetically pleasing homes.

These gigs offer a variety of ways to make extra money, turning your skills and interests into income streams. Whether you're a writer, designer, driver, or event planner, the gig economy provides opportunities for everyone. Choose the gigs that match your skills and interests, and start turning your time into additional income.

Conclusion

Be aware that financial success starts with changing your mind-set if you desire more wealth and prosperity. Each person who managed to become an independent one began their path with a little idea, which they turned into phenomenal. Investing also operates on this principle, starting small may be all it takes for your investment to blossom.

Dispelling the myth that one has to have substantial or significant wealth in order to create a sizable change or influence. Quite often, I have seen many people with huge deposits take their money and place it on a single high-risk stake which vanishes faster than it could be earned back. They might have been hard working, but they did not make a wise investment decision.

It is important to note that education and wisdom are critical when it comes to handling financial issues. Begin your financial journey early and learn how to get rid of procrastination, which does not only waste time, but displays lack of determination and mind-clarity.

One of the reasons why most people are unable to amass wealth is that they easily get swayed by other people's opinions. They give in to the opinion of the media and the conversations of neighbors around them hence, they waive off their judgment. It is important to bear in mind that opinions are the cheapest commodity in the whole world.

We all have more opinions than we know what to do with, and we are eager to force-feed them to whoever may be receptive. Letting yourself be guided by "opinions" will hamper your success in any venture, especially where you want to transform your goals into wealth. Should you allow other people's opinion to interfere with your own purpose it will stay unclear.

In the course of putting into practice the concepts suggested herein, choose what is right for you and stick to it. Feel free to share with your mastermind group only, but choose carefully. Choose those people with whom you share full hearts about your goals and dreams.

Friends and families mean well but they could be a hindrance to your improvement as people give you opinions which could be a veiled form of ridicule.

Some people have lingering feelings of insecurity because of an "expert" who has not understood how to say it nicely and whose so-called "opinions" were really a disguise for mockery. Remember always that you have a mind of your own, which you should use to arrive at your own conclusion.

To acquire this knowledge surreptitiously and guard your intent as you do so, if you need information or facts from others to make wise choices.
Desire is the beginning of all achievement in life. Retain this in your consciousness. A small fire produces little heat. Similarly, weak wants bring forth paltry results. In instances where you feel like you are not persistent enough, you may consider starting a bigger fire in your aspirations.

Self-discipline has been elaborated on in various previous chapters and is indivisible from the journey of transformation. Self-discipline is what your financial freedom and growth are based on. it gives you power over your thoughts, actions, and decisions. Therefore, once you come to the parting page of this book, it is high time to return to chapter one, follow the "Unleashing your potentials" instructions.

The zeal and persistence in which you will employ these directives will clarify how much you aspire to accumulate wealth. Therefore, if you encounter feelings of indifference then this means that you do not possess the "millionaire consciousness " needed while developing riches.

Just like water to the sea attracts itself to whosoever is mentally attuned to receive wealth. This book contains everything you need to know on how to make your mind attune into the calls which invite your desire. It begins by transforming. It's time to rouse from your slumber and take action, armed with the power of self-discipline. Your financial freedom and personal growth await you.

Reader Reviews

I hope you're enjoying this book. Your feedback is invaluable to me and will guide me in creating even better content for future books.

Your review can inspire and guide others on their journey to financial freedom and personal growth. I believe that together, we can create a community of empowered individuals ready to transform their lives.
It will also help me adjust and improve on the subsequent books.

Your opinion matters, and I appreciate your support!

www.ingramcontent.com/pod-product-compliance
Lightning Source LLC
Chambersburg PA
CBHW071154290526
45796CB00007B/39